January 19 2003

To Ch[...]

An oldie but goodie —
(published by and Editor-
in-Chief, family member,
JERRY MASON —

Congratulations, Eagle Scout —
Enjoy the great outdoors —
Love & Best wishes,
Judy & Mel Bender

SPORTS
ILLUSTRATED BOOK
OF THE
OUTDOORS

SPORTS ILLUSTRATED BOOK OF THE OUTDOORS

A Ridge Press Book

Text by John O'Reilly

Golden Press · New York

Editor-in-Chief: Jerry Mason

Editor: Adolph Suehsdorf

Art Director: Albert A. Squillace

Art Associate: Haig Adishian

Art Associate: Albert Kamp

Associate Editor: Ruth Birnkrant

Associate Editor: Evelyn Hannon

Editorial Assistant: Edwina Glen

Library of Congress Catalog Card Number: 59-14665

Prepared and produced by The Ridge Press, Inc. and the Artists and Writers Press, Inc. Printed in the United States of America by Western Printing and Lithographing Company. Published by Golden Press, Rockefeller Center, New York 20, New York

INTRODUCTION

In recent years, a phenomenal—and steadily increasing—number of Americans has become enraptured by the great natural world out of doors. What was once the province principally of the near-professional sportsman and athlete is now the park and playground of amateurs who simply wish to get out from under a roof and into the light, air, and space of a richly endowed land.

This book is for and about these amateurs. It is *Sports Illustrated's* record of the many pleasures and enthusiasms they are discovering for themselves and energetically pursuing in all the atmospheres, environments, and directions a three-dimensional world affords.

This vast and colorful shift in the living pattern of a nation has been of enormous and consuming interest to *Sports Illustrated.* For one thing, the movement has been going full tilt during all five years of the magazine's existence. For another, it involves the kinds of high-spirited, venturesome people and activity that thoroughly satisfy *Sports Illustrated's* definition of sport.

Americans are rarely an idle people, but the liveliness of our postwar years has made our pre-1945 pace seem positively lethargic. The economic well-being we have enjoyed for a generation has been accompanied by increased leisure time, increasingly spent out of doors. Today this movement has become the biggest boom in recreation ever to sweep this—or any other—nation.

If there are doubts about this, one has only to rise up on one elbow and look out over the edge of the hammock. The boat industry reports that some 37 million Americans currently are involved in pleasure boating, and a sweeping glance at the assorted craft on every damp spot across the country substantiates the claim.

In boating's wake is water skiing. Time was when this sport was practiced only by a handful of scatterbrained daredevils. Now water skiers are as thick as whirligig beetles on a mill pond. And how about skin divers? There are more than five million of these, and on any given day a large segment of the population can be found under water. Yet it was not so long ago that most persons thought skin diving meant bathing in the nude.

Contemplate bird watching. Bird watchers themselves used to be considered odd birds and were looked upon with suspicion. Today bird watching is a major sport with untold numbers of followers. It has to be ranked as a major sport when 8,000 enthusiasts turn out to take a Christmas bird census, as they do each December.

Hunters and fishermen are almost beyond counting. Campers and hikers invade the forests like the hordes of Tamerlane. In the West, there are more posses heading into the hills on trail rides than ever took out after desperadoes in the old days. The National Park Service reports that on the basis of current figures, 61 million persons will visit the national parks and monuments in 1959, and that by 1966 the visitor total will exceed 80 million. Beyond all these are other millions who strike for the open spaces each weekend just to get outdoors and do whatever strikes their fancy.

Accommodating all of these people and all of this activity are eight major geographical regions, eight environments, which are the splendor and loveliness of the land we live in—and the scenic background of this book.

Early Americans pushing across the continent encountered each of these environments in its pristine state. Emerging from the wide belt of forest that covered the East, they crossed great plains and ascended noble mountains which swept down, across desert and through fertile valleys, to the sea. To the North and South they found many kinds of country: meadowland, swamps and marsh, prairies dotted by lakes, and strings of coastal islands. In each habitat there was wildlife in profusion.

America's multiple and diverse environments have made it a land of limitless possibilities for recreation in the great outdoors.

It has been said that the impulse of the pioneer American confronted by a tree was to cut it down. There was so much of everything—so much land, so much water, so much animal life—that the thought of conserving any of it seemed ridiculous. There would be plenty for everyone, forever. Yet as the nation grew, its environments suffered. The natural abundance was plundered. The great forests of the Midwest fell before the lumberman's axe. Millions and millions of plains buffalo were slaughtered by the hide hunters. And thinking citizens realized with alarm that the nation's resources could, in fact, be exhausted. None too soon, national forests were set aside, and national parks, each located to preserve a certain type of habitat, were created. National wildlife refuges were established and each state developed its own conservation program.

Today the challenge is not only to conserve the environments we have become so used to visiting and enjoying, but to set aside new areas as well. For our population is increasing at a rate that will one day jam our recreation areas like New York's Times Square on New Year's Eve. That time is not yet; in fact, it need never come. But postponement of the evil day depends on the wisdom and care we apply to the future development of our environments.

Meanwhile, the following pages show venturesome Americans of all ages using and enjoying the environments of America. *Sports Illustrated's* best pictures of them in motion are accompanied by a text that draws on *SI* stories or research, but that has been tailored to the environmental organization of the book.

A final note: America's rediscovery of the outdoors is conferring many benefits upon the participants, not the least of which is a large and permanent increase in personal talents and abilities. Each of the many outdoor activities now available to us offers a handsome dividend in terms of skill or knowledge. Each of us who casts more accurately, negotiates the steeper slope, identifies an alien seashell or a new bird, rides the livelier horse, or comes about without losing headway, has gained in the process, is henceforward something more than he was.

Go out of doors and see.

*Beneath heaven's blue arch
lies the land. And of
all its temperaments and textures,
none is lovelier than sunlit
meadow and the green woods*

FIELD &

FOREST

*Young explorers stroll through lush wonderland of
Great Smokies on Tennessee–North Carolina border. This
is heart—and largest surviving area—of virgin forest that grew
from New England to Florida.* PHOTO BY RICHARD MEEK

*Frightened fawn (above) instinctively hugs
ground even when dappled coat does not blend
with surroundings. Couple dozing peacefully in forest are
perfectly camouflaged.* PHOTOS BY DON HORTER

Suppose that from a great height we are bending over the United States of America, inspecting it closely, as one would a map on a table. We can see the wide expanse of it and the fine detail at the same time. The first thing we notice from our vantage point is that for more than 300 years, man has been extremely busy changing the landscape to suit himself. We see that as a result of this industry much of the country is a patchwork of fields and woodlots, meadows and forests. In the flat or gently rolling parts the fields predominate. As the land rises the open areas become fewer and the trees take over.

This is the countryside as man has fashioned it to his own needs and uses. We do not have to look too closely to spot places where man has done a poor job. There are scars indicating the lack of planning or plain misuse. But, on the whole, the pattern is beautiful. If, with our sudden ability, we linger over it, we find that with each season it takes on new loveliness—the fresh green of spring, the kaleidoscopic hues of autumn, or the still white of winter. We shift our gaze from the woody hills and stone-walled fields of New England to the broad farmlands of the Middle

14 Atlantic states and the swampy woods and cotton fields of the

Deep South; then we look at the corn and wheat fields in the central part and on out to the forested mountains of the West.

Yes, man has done a lot of work here. But we are not looking for work. Heaven forbid! Our aim is to find man at play. We are trying to find out how he enjoys himself in the hours away from work. Our version of the outdoors is a place in which to relax and seek the recreation that field and forest have to offer. So we make another close inspection to see whether, after all this labor, man allows himself any opportunities for fun.

We begin assembling evidence from the start. Files of hikers with packs on their backs move along woodland trails. In open places and along the shore of lakes are the tents of campers. Some are on private land, but in the public preserves of the country, in national and state parks, there are thousands of campsites where families spend their vacations. As many as 18,000 young campers may be tucked away in the woods of the Palisades Interstate Park, a huge playground for city people, just up the Hudson River from New York.

It is apparent that camping is not as rugged as it used to be. Tents are made with screens and floors. Campers are using all manner of gadgets to add to the comfort of life in the outdoors: improved gasoline- and bottled-gas stoves, portable refrigerators, and foods easy to prepare. A few veteran campers scorn the use of modern gadgets in the woods, but most people are glad to adopt anything that makes outdoor living easier. One long-time camper friend of mine had at last weakened and bought some of the new camping appurtenances. As he sat in a light, folding chair after a meal cooked on a gas stove and eaten from disposable plates, he observed, "You know, these aluminum camp chairs aren't as repulsive as I thought they'd be."

Fishermen in high waders and battered hats adorned with flies seem to be on friendly terms with the world as they wade the streams. That new group, the sports-car clan, purrs along secondary roads. In a lonely clearing a man is building himself a log cabin. He goes about it with greater devotion than he ever lavished on repairing the roof or painting the porch of his home in town. On sunny afternoons, groups of oldsters pitch horseshoes at iron pegs. The work horses that supplied the cast-off shoes in the old days have become scarce. The shoes the players use now are manufactured solely for pitching purposes.

The draft horse may have given way to the tractor, but the pleasure horse is around in strength. Members of western riding clubs doll up their steeds and themselves in such finery that every trail ride seems like a parade. Some of the prettiest vistas are found on horse farms—those down through Virginia and Kentucky, in particular—but there are others from Florida to California. Mares with frisky foals grazing in lush pastures surrounded by board fences are deeply stirring sights.

Ponies have been staging a comeback and thousands of registered Shetlands are bringing prices higher than those paid for a good many horses. There is a creeping interest in donkeys as pets to keep in the smaller plots surrounding today's rural homes. The donkey, or burro, was once considered a fixture of the Southwest, but now he lives a life of ease in many eastern backyards.

The picnic is still a stable American custom, even when held in the backyard and called a "cookout." Often several families join forces and, in making their plans, repeat the oftheard words, "You bring the pickles and the potato salad. I'll bring the hot dogs and the rolls, and Aunt Annie will bring the soft drinks. We'll let the men bring their own." There is the organizational picnic of the East, where they still have the fat men's race, the sack race, and chase the traditional greased pig. And there is the big western picnic with people from miles about. They call it a "barbecue," but it's still a picnic.

18   Along toward the end of summer, county fairs spring up

Woodsmoke from log cabin in lonely clearing is nostalgic reminder of early settlers. Few old cabins exist today, but many people are building modern counterparts in a search for similar atmosphere. PHOTO BY KOSTI RUOHOMAA 19

across the nation. They are essentially outdoor festivals reflecting outdoor pursuits. The talk at these fairs goes like this: "Did you ever see such a big pumpkin? How do they get those pigs so clean? I couldn't keep the kids off that Ferris wheel, but I wouldn't ride on one of those things for a million dollars. Did you see those pickled peaches Mrs. Watkins won the prize with? My, I bet they taste good!"

Don't laugh at this talk as antiquated. Go to any county fair and you will find it as abundant as ever.

After the fairs have folded their tents, the hunters take to the outdoors to blast away at the cock pheasant against the blue, fall sky, the rabbit scurrying for the hedgerow, or the deer in the lower forty.

These are just a few of the recreations that people seek in the out-of-doors. As we study this mass search for fun and diversion, several things become evident. In the first place a lot of this outdoor play is harder than work. A man will tread a golf course until he is ready to drop, but will balk like a mule if his wife asks him to do something around the house that takes one-tenth the energy. Another will come near freezing to death in a duck blind and think nothing of it, but if somebody opens a window at the office his complaints about the draft are loud and bitter.

There must be few, if any, tangible rewards from these activities. I know a fellow who spends most of his money raising wild ducks and geese and then lets them fly away. Amateur ornithologists travel far and wide just to add names to the list of birds they have seen. A wealthy hunter with a lavish hunting lodge estimates that it costs him almost $1,000 for every duck he shoots. A man whose hobby is vegetable gardening avows that he will never do it again because he saves practically no money and it takes up too

much of his time. Yet the next summer finds him out there, toiling in the hot sun, fighting the bugs, and cursing the weeds. If he gets a few tomatoes or his sweet corn happens to survive, he goes around boasting as though he had invented agriculture.

There is also a sense of freedom involved in these outdoor pursuits. The man in the clearing doesn't have to build that log cabin. Nobody told him to do it and nobody can order him to finish it. It is his idea and he does it because he wants to. If the fellow who raises the ducks and geese wants to let them fly away, that's his business. If the country's fishermen were ordered to go fishing every Friday there would be an instant rebellion.

There are still other factors. Americans get a spiritual uplift as well as physical relaxation from the outdoors. The bulk of them may live in urban areas, but just let a pleasant weekend come along and they streak out of the cities like something was after them. Many—or most—of them may be content to enjoy a

Potential big game trophy, elegantly antlered moose hides in bush. PHOTO BY DAVID GOODNOW

drive in the country, but others seek greater rewards.

An affinity for woodlands is certainly an American heritage. When Joyce Kilmer wrote, "I think that I shall never see, a poem as lovely as a tree," he was expressing a feeling deep inside everyone. This nation was carved out of a forest. Those who were there to do the early carving derived their shelter, warmth, and much of their food and clothing from the things that the forest provided. The axe was the symbol of industry and well-being.

We talk now of pioneers of science and pioneers of industry and pioneers of this and of that. Almost everybody is some kind of a pioneer, but the word by itself brings a picture of sturdy men and women fashioning their livelihood in the wilderness; it recalls the log cabin in the clearing, the deer in the forest glade, the long rifle and the coonskin cap. It connotes fearlessness and self-reliance.

Whether most Americans realize it or not, there is something of that affinity for the forest hidden somewhere in their makeup. It could be that the wide acceptance of the picture window is an expression of it. It is too bad that under the crowded conditions of the urban sprawl now taking place in this country the picture window too often looks right into the picture window of the neighbor across the street. But somewhere in the vista the picture window provides there is a tree and that tree is the tree that Kilmer was talking about. It is also a small, green symbol of that mighty forest in which the nation had its birth.

Our folklore is full of references to the pioneers who carved a nation out of the wilderness, but there are few reminders of what that original forest was like. When driving through the broken patches of second-growth woodland in the eastern half of the country, it is hard to believe that this whole region was once covered with an unbroken, primeval, predominantly deciduous forest. It has been pointed out that if, in those times, a New England squirrel decided to go south, it could travel through this forest from tree to tree all the way to northern Florida without once having to descend to the ground.

23

Elk (or wapiti, meaning white deer), pushed back from home on plains by farmers and ranchers, is now mainly mountain animal in the West. PHOTO BY DAVID GOODNOW

Luckily, trees are a replenishable resource. With a minimum of management a cut-over area becomes a forest again. Although the generations that followed the pioneers continued to slash at the forests, it is astonishing how much woodland there is in the densely populated East. Mountain ranges are clothed with trees of respectable size, national, state, and county parks abound, and almost every farm has its woodlot.

The best place to get the feeling of what that original forest was like is in the Great Smoky Mountain National Park. Here are 507,159 acres of forest straddling the mountain ridges that form the border of Tennessee and North Carolina. Here that ancient forest reached its climax. This was its botanical heart. It took untold millions of years to reach that climax and, in view of what happened elsewhere, it is remarkable that there are 150,000 acres of this forest which have never felt the cut of the axe. It is the largest such tract in the East.

To this wilderness wonderland go three million people or more each year to share in the many pleasures it affords.

Through years of field study, botanists have recorded more than 1,300 flowering plants within its borders. Among them are 130 species of native trees. By comparison, the entire continent of Europe has only eighty-five. Nineteen species of the park's trees are represented by the largest specimens ever discovered.

Anyone who is the least bit mystified about what people find to do with their leisure time should take a summer tour through the Smokies. The place is alive with people, from Boy Scout campers to elderly picnickers munching sandwiches as they look out over the blue haze that gives the mountains their name. There are trout fishermen after rainbows in the rattling mountain streams, horseback groups on the trails, campers in every sort of

rig imaginable, bird watchers and hikers. Many go there just to look at the wildflowers.

When it's springtime in the Smokies these old mountains and the valleys between are clothed in a floral display so lavish and so varied that only those with hearts of stone could fail to be exhilarated. When late April brings the period to its climax, people come from many less-favored parts of the country to join the annual Spring Wildflower Pilgrimage.

What does one do on a wildflower pilgrimage? What makes it different from any other wildflower study? Such questions were answered for me the year I signed up and went along on some of these floral safaris. Flower watchers, generally speaking, turn out to be even more ecstatic than bird watchers. All age groups except tots were represented. They came from many places and many walks of life, but they all had the same enthusiasm.

There was no charge for any part of the pilgrimage program. Park naturalists and botany professors from several universities led the various groups to the richest flowering areas of the park. This was sometimes a difficult choice, for the Smokies put on their 27 flower show in profligate fashion.

On wooded slopes, white carpets of the fringed phacelia extend for acres. Cliffs overhanging mountain streams are festooned with red curtains of wild columbine. Seven species of trillium may be counted, and for those who consider a violet in the local woods to be the authoritative sign of spring, the springtime Smokies offer more than thirty species of violets in bloom.

To take full advantage of the resplendent displays, pilgrimage leaders arrange a variety of trips. Some are half-day jaunts, others take all day. You can walk, or ride, or both, and cameras are encouraged. You can pursue solitary fancies on a Ferns and Mosses Walk, or join a motorcade led by a ranger which winds through the park and stops every so often to permit close inspection of exceptionally fine concentrations of flowers.

One of the best walks is along the Porter's Creek Gap Trail. After a drive of ten miles, we left the cars and hiked into an area which contained some of the largest virgin forest in the park. Henry Lix, a park naturalist, walked at the head of the long file of pilgrims. Beneath that towering canopy we got a real feeling for the primeval forest. In single file we hiked up the winding trail beneath huge hemlocks, tulip trees, basswoods, and yellow buckeyes. Sunbeams came through their towering tops to throw spotlights on the ground cover. At one point Porter's Creek tumbled down the mountainside in a series of cascades. There was a long pause by the waterfall while the pilgrims went to work with their cameras.

Not all those who joined the pilgrimage were veteran wildflower enthusiasts. Many were vacationers who took this opportunity to learn something about flowers and at the same time to visit choice sections of the park.

28

1. *Missisippi Kite.* 2. *Tennesee Warbler.* 3. *Kentucky W.* 4. *Prairie W.*

Alexander Wilson, long before the renowned Audubon, painted birds in America from the Atlantic coast to the Mississippi.

Drawn from Nature by A. Wilson

Engraved by J. G. Warnick

1. Night-Hawk. 2. Female.

Wilson discovered, as well as painted, thirty-four distinct American bird species. COURTESY OF COLUMBIA UNIVERSITY

In the evenings we watched motion pictures and listened to lectures on the flora of the region, or gathered at wildflower clinics where the resident experts answered questions regarding plant identification and other mysteries.

After the spring wildflower pilgrims depart, their places are filled by other thousands. All year long, the Smokies put on a series of shows. One of the biggest crowds comes in June and July when the rhododendrons are in bloom. Here, again, these old mountains are lavish, for the park has 16,000 acres covered with rhododendron and laurel. If put into one patch, that would mean twenty-five square miles covered with these flowering plants. That is some wildflower garden!

Although the Smokies and other sections of the southern Appalachians represent the climax of the great eastern forest, there are many other places in the East where there are imposing stands of trees, representing numerous botanical associations. These range from the vast stretches of conifers in the North to the pine-and-palmetto association of the deep South. Our greatest forests, in extent and size of trees are, of course, in the West, but we will deal with them in a later chapter, for they are usually associated with mountains.

As the early pioneers penetrated the eastern forests, they encountered wild animals in great variety. Among the mammals there were creatures large and small such as they had never seen before. Some of them are no longer found in parts of their original ranges (the bison, before he was nearly exterminated, was found as far east as Pennsylvania), but others are now far more numerous than they were in the days of the settlers.

Today the eastern half of the country furnishes a more suitable habitat for some animals than did the unbroken forest.

Couples paddle warily around water lily patches on Rainy Lake. Pads become too dense for canoeing to

Patches of second-growth woodland, and open fields and hedge-rows, produce more sustenance than the sparse growth available in the shadow of a forest canopy. Take, for example, the Virginia, or whitetail, deer. The deer has always been an exciting animal in fact and fiction, but there are far more of them now than in the days about which most of the fiction was written.

In "the good old days" of the last century when there was no wildlife management, deer became woefully scarce in many regions. In the Eighties, when a lone deer was seen crossing the ice on the Hudson River, there were newspaper articles about the unusual occurrence. With the advent of game management, the deer were protected and hunting seasons were regulated. The deer proved highly adaptable. The woodlots interspersed with fields were much to their liking. They began to increase and kept on increasing.

Eventually, game management officials in many regions were faced with an astonishing fact. There were just too many deer. Population studies indicated that an open season on does was advisable. It took some time to get the people, even the hunters

34

tinue and they are forced to abandon water and portage through woods. PHOTOS BY WALLACE KIRKLAND

themselves, adjusted to the idea that this was a proper step in the management of the deer herd.

Doe seasons were established in many areas. Still the deer increased. They have multiplied in some regions to such an extent that many starve in hard winters for lack of browse. The bow and arrow, once the armament of small boys playing Indian, has now become an important weapon of the chase. Many states have a bow-hunting season for deer and in some thickly settled areas, such as New York's Westchester county, this is the only method by which deer may be taken legally.

In other areas they have a bow-hunting season, a buck season, and then an open season on antlerless deer, which means does and young bucks. Still the deer increase. Farmers complain about their ravaging crops, homeowners about their invasion of back yards to eat fallen apples. Nationally, the total annual deer kill is estimated at 1.75 million. In Pennsylvania it approaches 90,000 and still the herd increases.

In my section of eastern Pennsylvania, the opening day of deer season finds the hunters out in droves. They move into the 35

Primeval forest in Westchester County is home of bold fawn which leaves herd to examine relaxed vacationers. PHOTO BY GENE PYLE

Sun sets on summer day as horseshoe players have game among trees in Minneapolis city park. PHOTO BY RICHARD MEEK

state shooting-ground near my home by the hundreds, and at times it sounds as though a small war were in progress. Deer season passes, the woods become quiet, and when springtime arrives, it seems as though there are just as many deer as there were before. Non-hunters move into the woods to watch and photograph the deer and their fawns. It is a situation the old pioneers could never have believed possible—that there could be so many people and so many deer. It makes for tough problems in management, but there is no doubt that it is far better to have management problems than no deer to manage.

Perhaps it is just as well that the black bear hasn't proved as adaptable as the deer. It is difficult to imagine a modern commuter having his dash for the train made more exciting by the presence of a bear family. But given a break, bears do all right in the wooded mountains. Each year some 500 black bears are shot in the state of Pennsylvania. There are twenty-seven states which have regular open seasons on black bear and in seven of these hunting is permitted the year around.

In the deer, the bear, the panther, and the moose there is a range from the beautiful and dainty to the grotesque. Few more   37

Typical of rolling, verdant fields in East is countryside at Susquehanna Valley near Cooperstown, New York. Handsome thoroughbreds enjoy tranquil retirement on 5,000 acres of rich farmland. PHOTO BY RONNY JAQUES

bizarre creatures than the moose ever roamed anybody's woods. But as we go down the list in size, we find the eastern states endowed with some fascinating animals in the middle range.

From the days of the coonskin cap to the raccoon coat of the Twenties, and through the recent Davy Crockett craze, the animal supplying this fur has held a special place in the affections of people throughout its range, which includes all of the United States except the high mountains and deserts of the West. The raccoon may be a rascal, but he is a comical one. To me the raccoon is like Raffles, the famous safe-cracker of fiction, a cunning thief with an ingratiating personality.

I've been pestered plenty by raccoons. I've been outsmarted, duped, robbed, and scared seven-eighths out of my wits but, despite all I have suffered, I still have a tender spot in my heart for these masked footpads of the animal world.

One year I planted five varieties of sweet corn designed to mature over a long period. For once I was going to get my fill of those delicious ears. But the corn I got wasn't enough to put in a popular song. Just as it started to ripen, coons sneaked in under cover of darkness and ate the ears as fast as they developed. They would strip the ears from the stalks and devour them, leaving only the denuded cob with a rosette of shucks at the base.

And what happened to my bantam chickens that disappeared in the night? I haven't got proof, but I've got evidence. Who steals the frogs out of my pond? Don't think for a minute that it's Willie Sutton.

For a time I had the feeling that I had been singled out as the special victim of the entire race of raccoons. Then I discovered that my neighbors were in trouble, too. One nearby resident who had been bothered first with a beehive and then an army of

40

Spring in the magnificent Bluegrass country of Kentucky is scene of constant and vital interest in race horses. Future Derby winner may be in crop of frisky yearlings. PHOTO BY RICHARD MEEK

MG churns through mud spray in California version of English cross-country endurance trial for sports cars. PHOTO BY PHIL BATH

State Fair in Illinois provides night-and-day fun for all ages. PHOTOS BY RICHARD MEEK

squirrels in his attic began to hear sounds of larger game aloft. He discovered that he was host to a family of coons that gained access to the attic by climbing a tree and jumping to a window he had left open for ventilation. A tolerant man, he lived with them all summer.

Another neighbor was not so tolerant. He discovered that some shingles were missing from his roof and that a coon was going in and out of the hole. Knowing coons to be nocturnal, he had a carpenter repair the hole at night while the coon was out. The next morning some more shingles had been torn off and there was another hole. This happened three times before he found out that it was a mother coon and that she had three young ones in the attic. They had to tear still another hole in the roof to dispossess the family.

Numerous other instances of raccoon misbehavior have come to my attention. In New Jersey, a man who happened to be looking out of his window at two o'clock in the morning saw a brilliant flash from the top of a nearby high-tension-wire tower. As he described it, the flash was followed by a ball of greenish fire which dropped to the ground. A brush fire started, the man telephoned

46

an alarm, and sixteen members of the local volunteer fire department were routed from their beds to put the fire out. When the excitement was over, a search revealed the singed carcass of a coon beside the tower.

In Memphis, Tenneessee, a coon got into a television set. At Castleton-on-Hudson, New York, a coon short-circuited a high-tension wire and deprived 1,200 homes of electric power for half an hour. High-tension poles seem to have a fascination for them. A newspaper account tells of a pair of coons courting on high-tension wires in Iowa when they set off a blast of 6,600 volts of alternating current. The account explained that one coon was sitting on one wire and the other coon on another wire when they rubbed noses and closed the circuit with the resulting fiery tragedy.

All this and much other evidence indicates that the raccoon is not only here to stay, but appears to be increasing throughout most of its range. Most of them, of course, stay back in the woods and don't go around setting off electric blasts. In the springtime one is more likely to see him, after his nocturnal forays, spread out on a limb of a big tree, sunbathing. He lies there soaking up the sunshine and if he notices you at all, he looks down with an expression of indolent tolerance on that comical face with its black robber's mask. It's hard to stay mad at a critter like that.

Raccoons, like many other animals, pass through cycles of abundance and scarcity. Sometimes these fluctuations in population are local in nature, but at other times they affect the species throughout most of its range. The reasons for these natural cycles are not clearly understood. Nor is it fully understood why some species will extend its range and spread out over new territory. The spread of the coyote into the eastern states is hard to explain. Another case is that of the northward advance of the opossum.

49

Few animals are more fascinating than the beaver, to whom this nation owes a great debt. It was the search for the beaver that led to the opening up of much of the country in which we live today. The skunk, the wildcat, the porcupine are all fine residents of our woodlands, as well.

And then there are the many small mammals, the little creatures of the night that inhabit not only the woods and fields, but our yards and gardens. Few persons have seen the strange star-nosed mole, although it is one of the first things that European museums ask for when seeking specimens of American mammals. The flying squirrel, another oddity, has to be seen to be believed. The flying squirrel doesn't fly in the strict sense of the word. When it launches out from a tree it extends all four legs, spread-eagle fashion, and the skin folds tighten between the legs.

In this position it resembles a furry kite. The flattened tail is used as a rudder, giving the flyer considerable maneuverability. It can turn quite sharply to avoid limbs and tree trunks. As it reaches the end of its glide it turns upward and lands against a tree.

All of these mammals, from the moose to the mouse, serve to enhance our fields and woodlands. Even the man who devoted so much time and energy to getting the raccoon family out of his attic loves to tell about it every chance he gets. For those who would raise their eyebrows at the inclusion of the mouse among enjoyable creatures it must be said that even the house mouse has its attractive side. And if they can't stand house mice there are others, such as the white-footed mouse, the jumping mouse, and the meadow mouse, which prefer the outdoors.

Since the time of Alexander Wilson and John James Audubon this country has maintained a strong tradition in ornithology. 50 The bird life that inhabited the original forest was spectacular in

its variety and abundance. The passenger pigeon was so numerous that its flocks darkened the sky with their passing. The list of native birds included some of the finest game species to be found anywhere in the world—the wild turkey, the ruffed grouse, and the bob-white quail.

Some of these prolific flocks have since disappeared. The tragic slaughter of the passenger pigeon is an object lesson in sheer waste. The last passenger pigeon died in the Cincinnati zoo in 1914; the last official record of the Carolina paroquet is dated 1920, and the last heath hen failed to show up at its traditional mating grounds on Martha's Vineyard in the spring of 1933.

As in the case of the deer, many species of birds have prospered under the conditions created by man. The ivory-billed woodpecker may now be extinct in this country, but the slightly smaller pileated woodpecker appears to be adjusting itself and in many areas is increasing. Many songbirds are probably more numerous now than they were in the forest primeval.

Roger Tory Peterson, student, painter and photographer of birds, and high priest of the nation's bird watchers, has estimated that there are between five billion and six billion nesting land birds in the United States. Keeping track of this multitude is a growing army of bird watchers. Bird watchers range from the suburban or rural householder who maintains a feeding station and observes the birds from his window to the rabid compilers who journey the country over in search of more species to add to their life list.

Organized bird watching reaches its peak each year during the Christmas holidays when some 8,000 of the more ardent members of the fraternity take to wood and glen, marsh and field to make the Christmas Bird Count. The count, conducted under the aegis of the National Audubon Society in collaboration with the U.S. Fish and Wildlife Service, not only provides a competitive sport but produces much information on the habits and locations of winter bird species and populations.

52   Take, for example, the phenomenal activity displayed during

the 1955-56 count, when the group at Cocoa, on the east coast of Florida, won top honors for the entire nation. There forty-two watchers under the leadership of Allan D. Cruickshank ran up the massive total of 184 species, the greatest number ever attained on a Christmas Bird Count.

Cruickshank planned his campaign long in advance. The rules state that the count must be taken within one twenty-four-hour period from December 24 to January 2, in an area not greater than a circle with a fifteen-mile diameter. Dr. Cruickshank's region is rich in birds and he selected the cream of it. For weeks before the day of the count he and a corps of trained local observers studied the chosen area thoroughly, noting the movement of such rare species as avocets, white pelicans, and scissor-tailed flycatchers, so they would be able to spot them on the big day. Then he 53

picked his watchers with care. To increase his chances of a record
he imported some of the country's best bird watchers, among them
Peterson, who flew down from his home in Old Lyme, Connecticut. Other imports included Miss Farida Wiley, bird-trip leader
of the American Museum of Natural History; Dr. Joseph Howell,
professor of zoology at the University of Tennessee; and Henry
Bennett, supervisor of the Corkscrew Sanctuary. These, plus a
contingent of sharp-eyed local birders, gave Cruickshank a pha-
lanx which he divided into nine task groups.

Cruickshank had the manpower and he drove it unmercifully.
Each party was given a typewritten route annotated with the loca-
tion of nests, favorite feeding grounds, and other pertinent data,
and took to the field at dawn.

At noon watchers rendezvoused on a lonely back road and
gobbled their lunches while peering about unsuccessfully for the
seldom-seen western kingbird and scissor-tailed flycatcher. Then
they plunged back into the woods and marshes with orders to get
certain species missed during the morning.

All told, the Cocoa group spent over 500 man-hours in the
field, covered more than 1,000 miles by foot and car, and saw
almost 78,000 birds in achieving the record count. Greater importance always is attached to the number of species than to the
total number of birds.

The record count was made despite murky weather. Before
dawn a flashlight could barely pick out canvas-backs and pintails
through the dense fog. The watchers missed, for the most part,
the spontaneous burst of sound and color as thousands of herons,
ibis, and pelicans poured out of their rookeries at the first peep
of the sun.

54 But when the fog lifted in midmorning, they were gratified

by the vast numbers and varieties of ducks spreading out over the tidal lagoons as far as their 60-power Balscopes could reach. Further inland, Henry Bennett stumbled upon seventy-seven sand-hill cranes in one field, and in the pinewoods Peterson astonished even the other veterans by his remarkable ability to identify little-known birds by their calls alone. All those counted by ear were immediately confirmed by sight.

One rare accidental visitor Peterson picked up by sound was the pine siskin. Incidentally, seasoned birders never call out the name of a bird until certain of its identification. There is no more serious breach of birding etiquette than to be trigger-happy and name birds upon evidence which is too slight.

In late afternoon a sudden cold drizzle blew in from the Atlantic, but it turned out to be a blessing. Two parties parked their cars facing the surf and trained their binoculars through the rain at a fleet of twenty-six fishing boats making for the harbor under a canopy of screaming sea birds. They spotted over 100 gannets, a duck hawk, and, perhaps the best catch of the day, three parasitic jaegers, swift hunters of the deep, offshore seas, which snatch their food from the beaks and claws of other birds.

Cruickshank got the last bird of the day on a windswept tidal spit. While listening to Canada geese overhead he saw a lone silhouette streak down the sand spit.

"Green heron!" he shouted and added, by way of explanation. "It's easy to spot in silhouette because it's the only crow-sized heron."

All day long Cruickshank had been barking orders like a general dispatching crucial missions—"Get the old squaw"—"Honk up some fat geese"—"Tie down the avocets." And when his crew assembled at his home at Rockledge that night, his eyes were still

57

Elusive wild turkey is pictured in its natural environment. On 17,000-acre wild turkey preserve near McClellanville, South Carolina, wildlife biologist spent as much as ten hours a day in tiny blind waiting for wary turkeys to move into camera range. PHOTO BY HERMAN L. HOLBROOK

bright with the eagerness of the chase. Party leaders telephoned their tallies and the totals mounted. By 10 p.m. it became evident that the group had broken all Christmas Count records, and Cruickshank's grin was wider than ever.

The Christmas Count, of course, is only one of the many phases of bird watching. Call it a sport, hobby, a scientific pursuit, or what you will, it is a steadily growing activity that has added legions to those who share in the enjoyment of the outdoors.

There is yet another aspect of the eastern woodlands that brings millions of people out into the open. When October's bright blue weather comes along, the woods of eastern North America stage a mass color display unequaled anywhere else in the world. Millions take to the highways for a necessarily fleeting glimpse of this phenomenon of nature. It is a thrilling sight when viewed as a panorama, but still greater rewards come to those who forsake their cars and go for a walk in the woods.

Those who have not forgotten how to use their feet will do well to indulge in this old American custom. They will find that the fall forests, when seen from the inside, present new patterns in color and form at every step. An old stump wears a crown of emerald moss; the Virginia creeper hangs in cascades of scarlet; autumn leaves against the sky take on more delicate tints; leaf patterns on the forest floor become magic carpets, and even the scorned poison ivy assumes a brilliant beauty.

At this time of the year the weather usually co-operates with bright sunshine to temper the crisp air. When conditions are just right, it provides one of the more exhilarating experiences in nature. Going for a walk in the autumn woods is a custom that should be revived in the automobile age. It is good for the soul, it tones up the body, and it's all free.

Autumn in North America is time for cool golden days, change, and excitement. Children's imaginations can transform playground into a zoo, football field, or amusement park. PHOTO BY RICHARD MEEK

When winter comes to the northern part of these woodlands, they take on an entirely different fascination. Winter is a mysterious time in the woods and fields. Where do animals go and why? How do those who stay maintain themselves in these cold, lean times? There are the mysteries of migration and hibernation. For example, look ahead a few pages to the forlorn robin sitting on a fence of a Chicago suburb in midwinter.

This bird is not what he appears to be. You might think he is the first robin of spring, who took off too soon and got caught in a late-season storm. More likely, this is not the case at all. The robin probably has been around all winter and is waiting to migrate farther north. It's another one of those things about which   63 romanticists and scientists have divergent views and which even the experts admit they still don't understand.

Migration means a great shift in the robin population. Some of them nest farther north than others and some go farther south. Just what makes them go where they do and when they do has never been fully explained. There is a whole set of environmental and physiological factors that combine to make the robins move north in the spring. The increasing length of the day is believed to be a dominant one.

Whatever starts them off, the birds are ready for the long trip. Big deposits of fat give them the energy necessary for sustained flight. They are moved by a force they cannot resist. It

Beagles in full cry follow scent of hare cross-country in feverish moment of hunt. PHOTO BY JERRY COOK

brings them back to the place where they nested the year before. The males go first, for it is their job to decide where the summer home will be located.

When a male robin arrives in an orchard or yard, he lays claim to a territory with fairly definite boundaries. It is in this territory that the nest will be built. Then he proceeds to warn off other robins. To us it may be a song, but to the robin it is a proclamation of squatter's rights.

But there are other males about who dispute his claim. Those frantic fights you see on the lawn in spring are cock robins settling problems of real estate. And the robins that beat themselves against a window or the windshield of an automobile are not

always off their rockers. They frequently mistake their reflections for a territorial rival and try to drive him away. Remove the reflection and the bird stops this foolishness.

These fights between male robins are not lethal and I don't have any record of knockouts at hand. The robin is a light puncher, but his footwork is good. Dr. Howard Young, who has refereed many a robin match at the University of Wisconsin, points out that the cocks square off in four stances for ground attack: the tail lift, the crouch, the attack run, and the normal. In the tail lift the head is lowered and the tail elevated at an angle of about forty-five degrees. In the crouch the robin squats in threatening readiness. In the attack run the bird moves in low with knees bent. In the normal the bird stands upright and slugs without feinting.

When the females begin to arrive a week or two later the home territories are pretty well established. The singing is not primarily to attract the female. It does let the presence of a male be known, but it doesn't inform the female whether he already has a mate. The females blunder into the territories and are accepted by the males. Barring accidents, the pair remains together for the summer, and will rear two batches of young in the normal course of events.

When fall comes the miracle of migration happens again. The friendly robins on the lawn undergo changes. They no longer putter about the yard showing little fear of man. Instead they become wary. They gather in flocks and their whole attitude changes. Traveling at night in great squadrons, they join in the general compulsive movement of millions.

Our bird here in the snow is a central figure in a great mystery story. That mystery can continue to unfold as long as there

Forlorn robin, nearly obscured by midwest, midwinter snowstorm, may not be a southbound straggler but a local resident awaiting clear weather for migration farther north. Shifts in bird population are still a mystery to scientists. PHOTO BY ARTHUR SHAY

is a setting in which the action can take place. Speakers at a recent North American Wildlife Conference had some grim things to say about what is happening to that setting over a large part of the country. They painted an ugly picture of vast, sprawling urban complexes containing woefully inadequate green places for robins and for people; hardly any space for human beings to get out and cool off from the heat generated by the pressures of living in these contiguous cities.

The speakers emphasized how fast this condition is being reached in many areas. They told how superhighways, usually built through richer land, are spawning communities and industrial centers along their routes; how the rush to the suburbs results in cities bumping into each other; and how a population on wheels makes this urban sprawl possible. They pointed out that in less than twenty years the population of the United States has increased by fifty million and that there will be sixty-two million more Americans by 1975.

It is high time that the American people begin planning for green spaces in which to enjoy the relaxation and fun for which most of them work. Close by most communities there are still patches of woodland, there are marshes and ponds, meadows and streams. These remaining natural places have now become precious. In a short time they will be swallowed up by the urban complex and huge areas will lack outdoor living room.

It is time that the planners, backed by the citizens in each community, act to safeguard these sanctuaries. Not to do so will be to deny their outdoor heritage. For, as the physicist Dr. J. H. Rush put it: "When man obliterates wilderness, he repudiates the evolutionary process that put him on this planet. In a deep and terrifying sense, man is on his own."

68

*Here is a borderline
world created by the restless
union of sea and land*

SE

ACOAST

Once long ago I was a member of a group of yelling kids playing in the surf on the coast of Texas. The women folks, meaning my mother and my two aunts, were dabbling in knee-deep water, attired in the voluminous bathing costumes of the period. Hot sunshine beat down on a beach that curved off into the flat distance. The breakers rolled in across the wide shallows that are a feature of the gulf coast of Texas.

My uncle stood on the beach talking to a local rancher named Sam. It was Sunday and Sam, a tall, gaunt man with a black, drooping mustache, had spruced up a bit for the day. The boots he usually wore had been replaced by a pair of black, square-toed, ankle-length shoes. The trousers covering his long legs were dark and the jacket he wore was brown. He wore a white shirt, collarless, but modestly closed at the neck with a gold collar-button. Shading his aquiline face was a broad-brimmed rancher's hat.

At that time and place a man such as Sam would never have thought of putting on a bathing suit and going swimming, especially if there were women folks around. It just wouldn't have seemed decent. But as he stood there, talking to my uncle, he showed keen interest in the antics of us kids, nodding or waving   73 appreciatively as we emerged from the foam to see if our heroics with the breakers had been noticed.

The two men had quit talking and were just standing there in the sunshine when an astonishing thing happened. Simultaneously, Sam let out a wild yell and sent his big hat skimming up onto the sand. Then, with a roar like a charging lion, he ran into the water without even pausing to shed his coat. When he reached us astonished urchins, he began cavorting in the waves with the fervor, if not the grace, of a bull seal.

For the better part of an hour Sam was a sight to behold. He wallowed and tumbled in the waves in complete abandon, punctuating his gyrations with more yells. He would duck us kids two at a time and then we'd all gang up and duck him. It was obvious that he couldn't swim, but he made up for this deficiency with energy and spirit. Finally, we came out of the water, four skinny boys and a fully dressed but soggy man.

Sam went up to my uncle, the water squishing out of the eyelets of his black shoes, his mustache drooping more than ever. As he met my uncle's amused gaze, Sam registered deep embarrassment. What on earth had come over him?

"Ain't had so much fun in years," he muttered. His tones were both defiant and apologetic, yet at the same time his black eyes were bright with the exhilaration of the thing he had done.

Exhilaration is certainly the word for the effect that the seashore has on human beings and the vast numbers that hie themselves to the beaches these days are not shy about expressing it. Under the stimulus of wind and wave, people of all ages whoop it up in uninhibited fashion. If Sam could have been moved up a generation, he would shed his formal attire for a pair of trunks and become a skin diver.

The exuberating effect of the seashore on its human visitors is perhaps explained by the fact that it is one of the least-tamed of all natural environments. Even when it is flanked by a boardwalk and cluttered with carnival shows, the beach itself is still wild and uncontrolled. The power of moving wind and water is

"Bathing, Marblehead," by American Impressionist
Maurice Prendergast, captures ageless world
of waders escaping midsummer heat. Painting is
exhibited at Museum of Fine Arts, Boston.

boundless. The tide surges, the waves sweep the beach clean.

Because of their absolute exposure to the elements, beaches are quick-change artists. Any populous resort beach on a hot, summer Sunday is a place of colorful confusion. The human race, which comes in more assorted shapes and sizes than any other single species, is on hand in a vast swarm. Sunshine brightens the colors of beach umbrellas and bathing suits. The sea is blue and the combers erupt into white foam.

Odd forms of activity are in progress. Small humans are industriously burying their fathers in the sand. Mothers sit under sheltering beach umbrellas watching the interment. Schools of human fry splash in the shallows. Boys are staring at girls and girls are pretending they are not being stared at. The entire race is on the verge of starvation. It must be, for everybody is wolfing quantities of hot dogs, cotton candy, potato chips, and other things seldom included in the family meal at home. There it is, a kaleidoscopic mass of humanity, stuffing itself and expressing in many ways the exhilaration engendered by wind, sand and wave.

Then let a storm make up suddenly. Black clouds rumble in. Lightning cracks and rain falls in a summer downpour. Before this meteorological onslaught the human horde flees to shelter behind the boardwalk. Fathers pop out of their holes like sand crabs. Mothers frantically gather up lunch baskets and children, and the noisy exodus gets under way. There comes the mad dash across the rainswept sand, the shouts, yells, and calls to the reluctant young. The pavilions are packed with shivering, dripping crowds consuming hot dogs by the yard.

Behind them, the shore can hardly be recognized. In a few minutes, black clouds have turned out the sun and a gray gloom has replaced the bright scene of many colors. The waves have   77

Microcosmic intrigues of the shoreline
are missed by casual visitor. Calosoma scrutator,
green caterpillar hunter, wages struggle for
survival in sandy world. PHOTO BY JERRY COOKE

become bigger and angrier. The wind drives the rain and spin-
drift before it. Waves push higher and higher up the beach,
smoothing out the footprints in the sand and filling the holes from
which the fathers emerged so hastily. Except for sodden, over-
turned umbrellas and beach chairs, the beach is much the same
as it was before the human race was invented.

As famous and as populous as they are, the resort beaches
represent but a small part of the magnificent coastline of the
United States. From the ragged, rocky coast of Maine to the wide
beaches of Florida, around the great arc of the Gulf of Mexico
and along the miles of the mountain-flanked West Coast there is
an ever-changing littoral. In this domain, where the land and the
sea meet, people are engaging in all sorts of diversions beyond
lying on the sand or watching a bathing-beauty contest. There is
nothing wrong with either of these pastimes, but the bulk of the
populace demands more activity in its recreation.

An unsuspected aspect of the beach was unfolded to me when
I took the odd but fascinating photograph on page 79 to John C.
Pallister, entomologist at the American Museum of Natural History. Shapely girls, roving eyes, driftwood, sand crabs, empty
bottles, howling infants, and surfcasters are all common to beaches,
but this seemed to be something out of the ordinary.

"That," said Mr. Pallister, examining the picture, "is *Calosoma scrutator,* the green caterpillar hunter. It is a member of
the *Carabidae,* the ground-beetle family. It ranges over the entire
eastern United States, although in prairie country it tends to be
replaced by *Calosoma calidum,* which is black with golden spots.
Frequently it flies over water and drops in.

"This specimen could easily have fallen into the ocean and
got washed ashore; they can stand a lot of submersion. Or it could

78

have been running around on the sand hunting for food."

He raised a magnifying glass to one eye.

"It seems to have lost one tarsus—no, there it is. But it has lost a part of one antenna. Ordinarily, the green caterpillar hunter likes to climb trees for caterpillars. Inchworms are its favorite food. The grubs of this beetle live under leaves, humus, and beach drift, and prey on other insects."

"Do you find many insects on beaches?" I asked him.

Mr. Pallister smiled tolerantly.

"A lively place by day as well as night," he said. "There is plenty going on. The casual observer wouldn't see much. They're there, but you have to look for them."

Leaning back in his swivel chair and locking his hands behind his head, Mr. Pallister proceeded to give an entomologist's version of the seashore. Sometimes it was a grim picture, featuring death struggles in the insect world. At other times it was filled with bug song. There was intrigue and there was beauty.

It appears that the beach is a place haunted by insect predators. The great, gray robber flies sit on the sand, watching with bulging, expressionless eyes for something to move. When it does, they pounce with the fury of a saber-toothed tiger. Robber flies often catch their prey in mid-air. They seize it with their legs, plunge their beaks into it, and kill it with a potent injection. They even overwhelm bees, getting them from behind and knocking them out before they have a chance to strike back.

Dragonflies and damsel flies dance in the sunlight above the beach, while below them beetles crawl. It may be *Calosoma scrutator* on the prowl, but, more likely, wandering Colorado potato beetles, lady beetles, or weevils. Tiger beetles, some of them greener than emerald, are at home on the beach and nearby sandy areas. The larva of the tiger beetle has a neat trick for feeding itself. It lurks in a burrow with its head and mandibles just filling the surface opening. When some unsuspecting bug walks over it—whammo!—it snatches the victim in its jaws and retires for a subterranean meal. It also has hooks on its abdomen which lock into the wall of the burrow.

"In case it gets hold of something a little strong, it can't be pulled out of the hole," Mr. Pallister explained.

The entomologist finds his best bug-hunting in the drift thrown up by the tide. Farther on, in the fine, dry sand beyond the wave action, he finds the lair of the doodlebug.

The doodlebug, or ant lion, has a fat body and a large pair of pincers. It travels backward. When it digs its hole it moves in a circle, always traveling backward, until it has made a depression. Then it keeps tossing sand out of the bottom of the hole until it has formed a perfect, funnel-shaped trap of loose sand. 83

At the bottom of this pit the doodlebug lurks, completely hidden. When a scurrying ant or other heedless insect tumbles into the hole, it is unable to climb out again because of the bad footing on the walls of the trap. When it slides to the bottom, the doodlebug grabs with its pincers and pulls it to oblivion beneath the sand. Mr. Pallister likes doodlebugs.

"They make nice pets," he said. "You keep them in a box of sand and provide them with an ant occasionally."

Then he talked of the scarabs—the gold bug and the fig-eater —that drone over the beach at night; of the long-horned wood-boring beetles that bumble through the darkness in search of better wood in which to bore; of flies and fleas and mole crickets.

"The beach," said Mr. Pallister, "is a great place."

Leaving the strange realm of Mr. Pallister and his insects, you have only to move down into the region between the tides to find yourself in a world that is entirely different, but every bit as odd and fascinating. In this part of the seacoast many of the animals have adapted themselves to living part of the time in the water and part of the time out of it.

Barnacles, in many ways, are a nuisance, but when viewed as living organisms which thrive under rigorous circumstances they become objects of interest. When the water recedes they close tightly. When it rises again they open their shells and begin taking in the food the tide has brought them. They are completely adjusted to this ancient rhythm. If the tide failed to come in, they would die. Tide pools among the rocks teem with life which varies according to the region. Sea anemones open their fronds to become animated flowers; small fish dart in and out of crevices; starfish rest on the bottom and seaweed festoons the sides of the rocks. A person could spend a lifetime studying the world of the tide pools.

No beach is complete without seagulls and the shore birds that pace the wet sands for tidbits, always running daintily just beyond reach of the incoming waves. Bird watchers who live near the coast are lucky because they have both land birds and sea birds

*Driftwood fire is traditional
sight as beach parties gather in evening and
chilling salt breezes begin to blow.*

*New generations of young appear each year
to build in damp sand imaginary worlds of
tunnels and castles too soon destroyed
by rising tides.* PHOTOS BY JERRY COOKE

on which to train their binoculars. Along both seacoasts choice birding spots attract birders from all over the country. One of the most famous of them all is Cape May, New Jersey, to which generations of bird watchers have made pilgrimages.

Cape May is a focal point because it is a funnel for land birds migrating southward through New Jersey. When the migrators reach Cape May Point, they are confronted by the wide expanse of Delaware Bay. If they attempted to cross it many would be blown out to sea. Rather than brave the open water, therefore, they make a sharp right turn and follow the shore back, in a northwesterly direction, until the bay becomes narrow enough for them to cross safely and continue south.

This geographical circumstance attracts the bird watchers. During the height of the migration season groups of them sit on the dunes near Cape May Point observing the fantastic numbers of birds that make the turn and struggle against the wind. As many as 10,000 robins may pass through on a single morning, as well as thousands of other songbirds. Hawks of various species pass by in hundreds.

Through the joint efforts of nature and the U.S. Army Corps of Engineers, members of the boating fraternity are able to explore most of the coastal regions along the Atlantic Ocean and the Gulf of Mexico without having to venture offshore. The longest stretch of this Inland Waterway reaches southward from Norfolk, Virginia, 946 miles to Miami, Florida. Down below Miami, visitors by boat or car come upon that unique part of all American coastal environments, the Florida Keys.

The keys, of course, are islands, a chain of ancient coral reefs curving southwest from the tip of the Florida mainland for a hundred miles to Key West. Because the main line of keys is

1.*Roscate Spoonbill*.　　2.*American Avoset*.　　3. *Ruddy Plover*.　　4.*Semipalmated Sandpiper*.

*Wide, sandy coasts and surging seas at the
Hamptons on Long Island Sound
provide varied pleasures for small fry. To those
aboard plastic, air-filled rafts (above)
thrilling dangers lurk in each swelling wave.
For others (left) excitement can be found in foamy
remnants of spent wave.* PHOTOS BY TONI FRISSELL

connected by a broad highway that enables the visitor to travel their entire length by automobile, it seems proper to consider them a part of the seacoast. It is an astonishing part, for the keys have no resemblance to any other section of the coastline.

Although, technically, they are in the subtropical zone, they are tropical in every sense of the word: in climate, in vegetation, in appearance. Most of the things that grow there in the wild state come from the West Indies, the Bahamas, or Mexico. If the visitor stops his car to inspect the jungle that grows beside the highway he will find hardly anything with which he is familiar. Instead, he will encounter mahogany trees, odd gumbo limbos with bark like peeling varnish, pigeon-berry trees, poisonwoods, and wild coffee bushes.

The color of the water surrounding the keys varies from the sharpest aquamarine to the deep blue of the Gulf Stream, which flows beyond a barrier of coral reefs. And when roving squalls churn the shallow waters of Florida Bay, the action stirs up the marl—the pale mud—on the bottom, so that after the squall passes the water is milky white. It remains that color until the marl settles, when it becomes aquamarine again.

These tropic isles are strung along the Overseas Highway like colorful beads on a string. The old railroad which connected Key West with the mainland was washed out by the great hurricane of 1935. It has been replaced by this modern highway, tying the keys together with concrete bridges up to seven miles long.

They call the trip down the keys "going to sea in your automobile." Most visitors traveling this route have fishing as their main objective. And well they might. The Florida Keys boast that they have "the finest fishing in the world." This may or may not be true, but there are so many different kinds of fish in these 91

waters that few visitors are inclined to argue the point. In the
region are found more than eighty species of fish that will bite on
a hook.

Here fishermen don't even have to have a boat to catch salt-
water fish. Wooden catwalks attached to the sides of the bridges
offer vantage points for hauling in a big variety of fish. There
was a time when people stationed themselves directly on the
bridges, but as traffic increased, this was discouraged. If a fisherman got a big bite and stepped back into the roadway just as a
speeding car was coming along, it not only spoiled the fishing,
but sometimes spoiled the fisherman, as well.

Any weekend finds all manner of fishing in progress along
the keys. Some anglers drop their lines from the catwalks; some
hire outboard motor boats to carry them into sheltered channels
or out in Florida Bay. Some hire guides to take them after that
speed-demon of the shallows, the bonefish. Small charter boats go
after bottom fish along the reefs, while in the Gulf Stream beyond
are larger boats in pursuit of marlin, wahoo, and dolphin. To see
all this activity, as well as the steady stream of motorists hauling
their boats, makes it easy to believe the boast of the keys—"the
best fishing in the world."

Not all those who roll down the Overseas Highway are on
fishing trips. The exotic bird life and other aspects of this touch
of the tropics are bringing thousands of visitors. Wading birds
are a specialty of the keys. The heron family is represented by
many species, from the little blue heron to the great white heron,
which, in fact, is found *only* in this general region.

In the springtime, motorists become excited at seeing brilliant pink birds feeding in sloughs not far from the highway.
92 Many mistake them for flamingos because of their color, but they

On California's Monterey Peninsula, not far from beach-lined coast, beautiful Laguna Seca race track, situated on dry

offers exciting course for sports-car devotees who crowd the sandy hillside to watch. PHOTO BY SAM AND JIM VESTAL

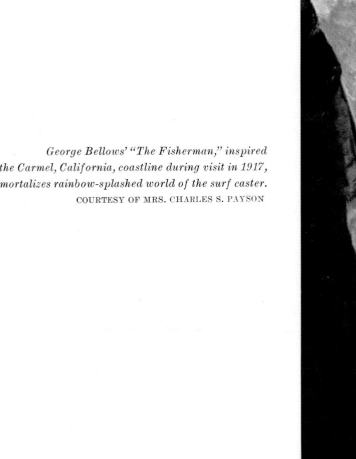

are the smaller roseate spoonbill, which nest on keys out in Florida
Bay and bring their young to the sloughs to feed.

The more ardent bird watchers come in groups to Tavernier,
on Key Largo, where they take bird tours run by the National
Audubon Society out into Florida Bay. Many a bird watcher on
such a trip has added several birds to his life list in one day.

These usually include the bizarre roseate spoonbill which
feeds by waving its paddle-shaped bill in the mud, and the reddish egret, that restless member of the heron family, the most
impatient fisherman of all. Instead of standing motionless until
a fish comes along, as is the custom of most herons, the reddish
egret moves across the shallows in a succession of erratic dashes,
96 hurrying this way and that, to snatch up small fish. It would

seem that the bird expends more energy than it acquires from the fish it consumes.

Some visitors go to the keys to study the tropical plants that grow there, including species that are found nowhere else in the United States. And it appears that uppermost in the minds of some is the prospect of indulging in two of the food specialties of these islands: turtle steak and key lime pie. Some people can pass up turtle steak, but others become addicts. The key lime pies are made from the small, juicy, tangy, thin-skinned limes that grow on the keys. There are certain perennial winter vacationists who eat key lime pie every day they are on the keys.

But if we were to consider eating as a part of outdoor activity this book could go on indefinitely. How about those crisp, 97

young, softshelled crabs of the Eastern Shore? How about those Olympia oysters of the West Coast and how about catfish and hush-puppies in the Deep South? Let us not wander into such gastronomic bypaths.

On many beaches, particularly southern ones, young people and old spend hours walking slowly along the beach with heads bent over and eyes on the sand, as though searching for something they had lost. These people are indulging in the old shell game, another one of the habit-forming pursuits a beach affords.

Seashells are the external skeletons of mollusks, a lowly class of animals that has the ability to produce these jewels of the sea, some of them as beautiful and as delicate as any trinket fashioned by man. There are about 80,000 known species and some 500 new ones are being discovered every year. Billions of shells are washed up on the world's beaches each year, but only a small percentage of them makes the trip in prime condition. The abrasive action of sand and water dims their colors and wears parts of them away. This adds spice to the game, for the collector has to pore over thousands of fragments to find one or two beauties intact.

Most visitors to such beaches have done a little casual shell collecting at one time or another. Their collections usually wind up in a shoe box stored away in the attic. Serious collectors not only spend all the time they can combing the beaches, but also trade and buy shells from all over the world. Fancy shells generally come from warm waters. The west coast of Florida has good shelling beaches, particularly at Sanibel Island, off Fort Myers. On the Pacific Coast, shell collectors journey to the beaches of Magadelena Bay, on the southwest coast of Baja California.

Whether they are hunting shells, swimming, or lying on the sand, the majority of summer vacationists at beaches is intent on 99

getting a good coat of tan. They devote so much attention to it that it apparently becomes the prime objective of their holidays. Getting a coat of tan has become an American fetish. The city girl goes to the shore for her vacation and while there rubs herself with assorted lotions and creams intended to bring out that rich, golden color. She devotes long hours to turning and roasting her anatomy until it has reached the glowing point.

Nicely fried, she returns to the city where her friends and all the people at the office say, "My, what a lovely coat of tan you've got." The brown one passes off the compliments on her tawny epidermis as though she was that color all of the time. But in a few short days she fades back to her original color and the ritual is over until the next summer. And don't think this custom is indulged in only by females. There's many a man who devotes almost as much attention to tanning his own hide and who passes off the compliments with just as much secret delight. This custom is now so deeply rooted that it is hard to believe that women once wore poke bonnets and long-sleeved gloves just so they wouldn't get all brown and spoil their lovely complexions!

In like manner, the boating habits of the nation have changed.

Wherever you go along the seacoast—in bays, sounds, and canals—there are boats. Not boats in the old-time sense, but in the new: craft in assorted shapes, sizes, and types; outboards, catamarans, class sailboats, houseboats—every sort of rig imaginable. Some of them don't look like traditional boats at all, but have tailfins, like automobiles. To keep up with the needs of the growing boating fraternity, marinas are springing up along the coasts. These are marine communities with docking space, supplies, groceries, and a host of other facilities. East Coast or Pacific Coast, it is the same.

Among the first major facilities built for visitors to the Everglades National Park is a new marina which prides itself that it can take care of any type of boating enthusiast likely to come along. A man can bring his boat on a trailer and launch it. He can bring the motor and rent the boat, or he can bring the boat and rent the motor. He can rent the whole rig or he can pay for a ride in a boat.

If he comes in his own boat he can find dock space, marine-gas pumps at the dock, a grocery store, fishing-tackle shop, restaurant, cocktail lounge, motel, trailer park, and benches where he can sit in the sun and think. These super boat basins have sprung up with the increase in boating and, like supermarkets, they are getting fancier and fancier.

In the same way, towns along the coast which have good boating facilities are growing rapidly. As an example take Newport Harbor, California. Twenty-five years ago, Newport Harbor was a small, rather remote resort, an hour and a half from Los Angeles. There a few Starboat sailors, a group of Snowbird skippers, and a few cruising men raced against each other, frequently bumping into the sand bars that laced the shallow channels.

Now, on any weekend throughout the year, no fewer than 4,000 101 yachts, worth probably $30 million, are jammed into 700 acres of mooring space. The quiet little town has grown into a bustling community of 35,000. The channels in the main harbor have been dredged straight and deep to provide passage for every conceivable type of pleasure boat. The sand bars have been filled and developed into a complex of islands, canals, and private piers. When they hold the race to Ensenada, Mexico, a flotilla of yachts numbering between 200 and 300 sails out of the harbor—and that is just one of a calendar of year-round regattas.

All along our coasts harbors are teeming with boats. New harbors are being built and existing facilities are being improved through dredging. Every available beach is also being developed to accommodate the vacationists' insatiable need for sun and sand and sea.

The obvious stumbling block in this situation is that, although the population keeps growing at an ever-increasing rate, the good Lord isn't making any more seacoast. With his dredges and his draglines man can improve or rearrange sections of it to fit more closely to his needs, but the seacoast that we have now is all we'll ever have. It is up to the American people, then, to use their beaches, bays, and harbors to the best advantage.

With outdoor recreation now recognized as one of the primary needs of the people, cities are making efforts to keep their nearby waters pure and clean. New York City has spent hundreds of millions of dollars in a long-term program to make its surrounding waters and beaches healthy places, to be enjoyed by the millions crowded into the metropolitan area. Federal and state bodies are making studies to determine how much more coastline may be set aside for purely recreational purposes.

As the experts make their studies and surveys, the bathers on the beaches, the fathers buried in the sand, the patient surfcasters, the boat owners, the shell collectors, and the kids building castles at the edge of the waves are all becoming more and more numerous. It is to be hoped that the outdoor recreation

planners can keep up with them.

SWAMPS

Vivid as a night bird's cry and profusely alive from treetop to bog bottom, our native wetlands are now being discovered by wide-eyed visitors

&MARSH

In the Everglades National Park a while ago, the management
built a boardwalk into a swamp, thinking that some visitors might
like to get right in there and see the plants and animals at first
hand. In the beginning it wasn't much of a project, just a short
walk with a wooden platform at the end. They named it Anhinga
Trail, after those birds with the snaky necks that are more at home
under the water than they are in the air.

It wasn't long before the Anhinga Trail ranked as one of the
more popular features of the whole park. People not only left
their cars and entered the swamp, but many stayed for hours
watching and photographing the big alligators that came to take
handouts, the gaudy gallinules tripping across the lily pads, and
the gars that swam in the water just below their feet. They
watched a snake catch a fish, trained binoculars into the tangled
growth in search of shy birds, or listened to a frog chorus.

They came in such numbers and lingered so long that the
original boardwalk had to be rebuilt and enlarged. I know one
man who had never been in a swamp in his life, but after discovering the excitements and pleasures of the Anhinga Trail he spent
his afternoons there whenever he could.

Most people have a mental picture of a swamp as a dismal, gloomy place full of stagnant water and inhabited by all sorts of creepy things, a place to stay away from. I'm afraid such people never have been inside a first-class swamp.

The initiates learn that a swamp is a place of somber beauty, a lush environment where plants and animals thrive in super-abundance, a dramatic wildlife habitat where action, sometimes grim and sudden, takes place every part of the day or night; a zoo without cages and a botanical garden all done up in one package.

The ranks of the converted are growing, thanks to the Anhinga Trail and similar facilities which have been provided to enable people to penetrate swamps without getting bogged in them. On the other side of Florida, twenty-five miles southeast of Fort Myers, local residents and wealthy philanthropists gave their time and money toward a project of the National Audubon Society to save the Corkscrew Swamp, which contains one of the last large stands of big cypress trees.

After acquiring the land, they established the Corkscrew Swamp Sanctuary. Into it, the Society built a boardwalk more than half-a-mile long. It is a sturdy, winding walk with railings on both sides and occasional lookout points with benches. It has been as successful as the Anhinga Trail. Visitors from all over the country stroll leisurely along, taking in sights they have never seen before. Samples of the rich Florida bird life fly over their heads, roost in trees, or wade the brown swamp water. Here, too, alligators have become accustomed to boardwalk strollers and sprawl inertly on logs to be photographed.

Two features of this swamp hold special interest for visitors. It is a favorite nesting place of the wood stork, the only true

108   stork inhabiting the United States. In the early spring thousands

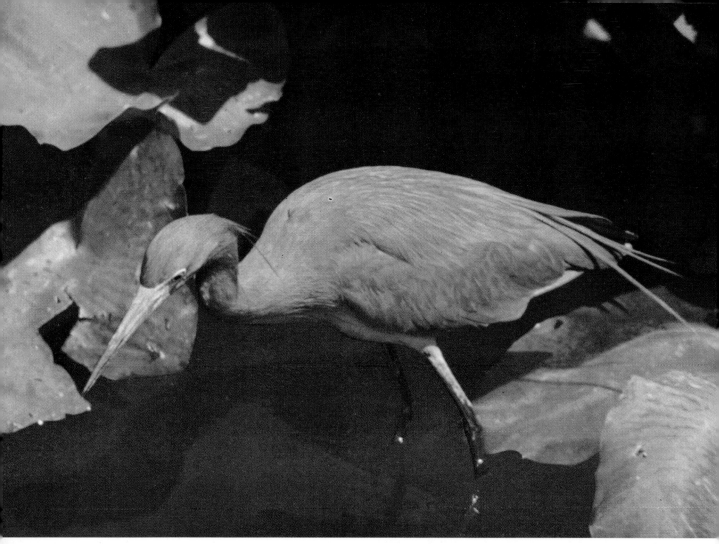

Posing motionless, delicate Little Blue Heron contrasts sharply with lush, wilderness setting.

of them nest in the tops of the cypress trees. It is also a great place for wild orchids, which bloom from April through June. There are at least ten species of epiphytic orchids, which are most abundant around the custard-apple ponds where they festoon the tree limbs with hanging gardens. Terrestrial orchids are found in the wet prairies bordering the swamp and along the edges of cypress heads.

Within this swampland sanctuary the old cypress trees stand in a curving horeshoe five miles long and from 400 yards to three-quarters of a mile wide.

As one of the early visitors to the sanctuary, I joined Henry P. Bennett, the Audubon Society warden, and Sam Whidden, who has lived all his life at the edge of the swamp, for an afternoon stroll along the boardwalk. Here was a new type of boardwalk, vastly different from those at ocean beach resorts. This was a place of restful beauty. Here are some notes I made as the three of us meandered through Corkscrew Swamp:

*Fighting over fish dinner or roosting quietly
in the mangroves, Brown Pelicans provide comic relief for
visitors to coastal areas.* PHOTOS BY DAVID GOODNOW

Wood Ibis (above), only American stork, is seen near rookeries, clusters of thousands of nests. His ungainly form when grounded stretches to graceful pose in flight.

Body submerged, neck extended, Anhinga (left) seems most unconventional bird, but amphibious antics facilitate catching fine fish quarry.

Nervously twitching tail gives stern-eyed Purple Gallinule (far left) a pompous air as he stalks prey of frogs and snails.

PHOTOS BY DAVID GOODNOW

"Cypress trees tower up to 150 feet. American egrets making an awful racket. Boardwalk enters lettuce lakes — opening in swamp covered with water lettuce. Wood storks flying back and forth almost constantly. White ibis feeding in slough and flying a third of a mile to where they're nesting. Several wood storks stop and pose on dead tree, looking like a Japanese print. Limpkins squalling deep in swamp. Spanish moss streamers wave in faint breeze. Flocks of red-wing blackbirds pass overhead. Snowy egrets fly over in close formation on way to roost. Great blue heron calling in distance, sounds like somebody being murdered. Fish crows fly over. More white ibis sail over our heads. American egrets quit feeding and fly over lettuce lakes. Alligators lying motionless on logs. Sam says one is Old Rusty. All look alike to me. Gars splash in brown water. Pileated woodpecker whams at tree. Wood duck flies right in front of us. Green frog calls. Florida gallinule sails in, lights on piece of water lettuce and skids like a bird on water skis. Anhinga (water turkey) sits on limb with wings outspread. Dusk gathering now. In distance sandhill cranes set up rolling call. Darkness thickens. Screams, squalls and splashes sound from swamp."

As we sat there in the gloom listening to the swamp sounds around us, Sam said, "There's some nice scenery in this swamp and it's going to be here a long while now. It does your soul good just to sit and look."

Florida has a wealth of such regions and the people of the state are beginning to realize how valuable they are. Years ago there was an abortive attempt to drain the Everglades in the hope that they could be turned into valuable crop lands. The project resulted in near disaster. Drought hastened the process. Fires started and spread over hundreds of thousands of acres. 115

When the wind was right, tourists found Miami enveloped in smoke clouds. The water table dropped and salt began to show up in water systems. Government action was taken to stop the drainage and put the water back on the Glades.

Where the great fires once burned is now the site of the Everglades National Park, a million-and-a-half acres composed mostly of swamp and marsh. Between the inland fresh-water marshes and the coast is a tangle of mangrove swamps. Stretching in a wide band along the west coast is the finest mangrove forest in the world, the trees attaining a height of more than seventy feet and rising in a dark green mass above the impenetrable tangle of their grotesque roots.

It was my good fortune to spend a week with Barnie Parker, a rugged ranger, whose job is to protect the wildlife in 300,000 acres of this wild country. Barnie has the remotest station in this swampy wilderness and patrols his area in the Green Hornet, a stocky outboard skiff painted green and brown like the mangroves. During my week there I went with him.

On these trips we moved up the big tidal rivers—Lostmans, Rogers, the Broad, the Shark, and the Harney. Leaving the rivers we followed winding creeks and crossed wide bays. The mangroves, lovers of salt water, dwindled in size and finally disappeared altogether as we pushed inland. Then we would be gliding between banks covered with thick sawgrass. By standing up in the boat we could look out across the endless sea of grass, dotted with clumps of trees called hammocks. This was the Everglades, a watery plain like no other part of the United States.

Warm climate and abundant water provide ideal conditions for other famous swamps of the South. High on the list is the Okefenokee, of Georgia, 600 square miles of cypress, waterlogged

116

Prepared for escape to water, not to air, Anhingas perch in favorite roost—low trees and bushes. PHOTO BY DAVID GOODNC

Barking tree frog, Hyla gratiosa *(above), can change skin color, depending on environment.*
Goliath among tree frogs, Texas-Mexican Hyla baudini *(right) often grows three or more inches long.*
Hyla eximia *(below) are also changeable, hail from Mexico.* PHOTOS BY CHARLES M. BOGERT

prairies, and islands. Aside from the many other wonders of this great swamp, it is noted for two things in particular: it is the source of the Suwannee River and the place where cartoonist Walt Kelly's collection of critters, headed by Pogo Possum, lead their eccentric lives. It is too bad that Virginia's Great Dismal Swamp, with an area of 700 square miles, isn't cheered by a similar family of loquacious denizens.

Speaking of loquacious denizens, frogs utter the true voice of the swamp and fresh-water marsh. During the breeding season millions of them assemble and yell their heads off in a mighty chorus. As many as ten or more species may be sounding off at the same time, filling the night with their ancient song. They may be heard in the Pine Barrens of New Jersey, in the lowlands of South Carolina, or anywhere else where there is abundant shallow water. Even the frogs and toads that live on land or in the trees head for the nearest swamp, marsh, or pond to sing their love songs in the spring.

More spectacular and certainly more important are the millions of waterfowl that breed in the extensive marshes of the northern United States, including Alaska, and Canada. Augmented by the families they have raised, great flocks of migratory ducks and geese move southward each fall to the coastal and inland waters which are their winter homes. These migrating millions constitute one of the most thrilling aspects of all American wildlife. Whether looked at from a purely esthetic point of view, as a gourmet's delight, or as providers of outdoor sport, the migratory waterfowl are an international asset beyond estimate in terms of dollars.

At times this asset has been threatened. Back during the great drought of the Thirties, the continent's waterfowl population reached a perilously low point. Excessive drainage and lack of rainfall had reduced its breeding grounds and dried up many of its wintering areas. Through a concerted effort by governmental and private organizations, a campaign was launched to bring back the ducks. The system of National Wildlife Refuges was in-

creased to more than three million acres. Projects were started
to put water back on the breeding grounds. Dams and dikes were
built to retain what water there was. Then the rain cycle returned,
the marshes filled again, and the waterfowl responded. Their
numbers increased rapidly and millions again took to the air.

Prominent among the migrating hordes is the Canada goose,
an inspiring bird which many claim to be the noblest of all waterfowl. A man doesn't have to be a hunter or a bird watcher to
be stirred by the sight of a great V of Canada geese honking high
in the sky. Those pointed wedges and those wild cries in the
spring mean that each formation is heading back to the very
meadows, marshes, or ponds where they were hatched and reared.

Because they return to the same area each year to breed, the
species has developed many distinct races. The term Canada
goose applies to strains ranging in size from big twelve-pounders
down to little birds about the size of mallard ducks.

As migrating time approaches in the early spring, the geese 123

Noblest of all waterfowl,
the Canadian goose wings homeward to
meadows where he was hatched and
reared. The annual pilgrimage
of honkers assembled in traditional
V-shaped wedge is stirring sight
against blue spring sky.
PHOTO BY JOE VAN WORMER

At sight of intruders, some 3,000 snow geese desert their feeding grounds for sanctuary of flight.

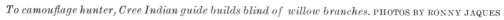

To camouflage hunter, Cree Indian guide builds blind of willow branches. PHOTOS BY RONNY JAQUES

126

assemble in flocks on their wintering grounds. They honk and
gabble to each other. An air of restlessness is evident. Then a part of
the flock will rise into the air and head north.

On their breeding grounds they display distinctive traits.
They mate for life, but if one of a pair is killed the survivor may
take another mate. Geese are among the few species of birds in
which the family group remains together after the young are
raised and are able to shift for themselves. When fall comes they
migrate together and remain together on the wintering grounds.
It is not until they are back on the breeding grounds the next
year that the young geese leave to establish families of their own.

Remaining together in family groups for a whole year is also
a trait of the whooping crane, America's tallest bird. The whooper
is to the wading birds what the Canada goose is to the waterfowl.
During the last twenty years the entire population of wild whooping cranes has shifted from a low of fifteen to a high of about
three dozen. Each year this little band of big birds makes the   127

long and hazardous trip from its breeding grounds just south of Great Slave Lake in Canada's Northwest Territories to their wintering grounds at the Aransas National Wildlife Refuge on the Texas coast.

So much has been done by the governments of the United States and Canada, by the National Audubon Society, and by other organizations and individuals to keep this remnant of a great race flying that the whooping crane has become a symbol of the great open spaces of America. Each fall when all the families have returned to the Texas coastal marshes, a careful count is made and newspapers over the country report how many young have been brought back and whether any of the old birds are missing.

This nationwide interest in the welfare of the whooping cranes is an important milestone in conservation. It proves that the American people can extend themselves to save a creature whose importance far exceeds mere economic value.

It is also a healthy sign that so much effort is being put into saving existing swamps and marshes and into creating new ones. A few years ago the U.S. Fish and Wildlife Service made a detailed survey of the nation's wetlands, including swamps, marshes, bogs, wet meadows, potholes, and sloughs. Their report disclosed that although millions of acres of wetlands had been lost through drainage, much of it unwarranted, the country still has 74,440,000 acres of such wetlands, which are of value in the production of waterfowl and which have a growing number of economic and recreational uses.

After visiting the whooping cranes both in the wild pond and marsh country of Canada and in the Texas marshes, and after many hours spent in the company of wildlife in some of the finest swamps our country affords, I must admit to a certain prejudice. It would be all right with me if half the country were nothing but swamps and marsh.

128

In still of early morning, the hunter waits, completely concealed by natural blind of tall reeds which line Texas lake front. His decoys are barely visible in the dim setting. PHOTO BY DMITRI KESSEL

MOUNTA

The stern and
cloud-cloaked peak
is for all men
below a comfort and
a challenge

INS

Out on the plains of Kansas, where the flat land stretches away into the hazy distance, an elderly codger was telling about a trip he had made to California. He avowed that he didn't like it.

"Everywhere you look in that country," he said, "there's nothing but a lot of dern mountains sticking up to spoil the view. Why, around here a man can see for forty mile."

This attitude toward mountains can be considered exceptional. People regard mountains with different emotions, but the reaction is almost never one of aversion. Usually, mountains are regarded with awe. Their massiveness, their ruggedness, and their inaccessibility command respect. To many persons they present a challenge. Most of us, on gazing at some towering height, get the feeling that it would be wonderful to be up there, to stand proud and strong on that mighty pinnacle, surveying the world below.

People who live in the mountains, or near some particular mountain, regard them with intense local pride, upholding their beauty and magnificence with all the ardor of a man boasting about the local fire department. They develop strong affection for their mountains and speak of them as though they were old neighbors, something more than stone and earth. Once I saw a native of Lake

134

Placid, New York, fly into a towering rage when a visitor from the West referred to Whiteface Mountain as "that hill out there." Whiteface is 4,872 feet high.

My dictionary describes a hill as smaller than a mountain and a mountain as larger than a hill, but it doesn't point out the dividing line between the two. Westerners living within sight of the mighty Rockies probably can be pardoned for referring to eastern mountains as "hills," but in the Appalachian chain are ranges which have charm and beauty of a sort quite different from that of the western ranges. Easterners wanting to pursue the argument can say, "Your mountains are bigger, but ours are older."

The Appalachians came into being 200 million years ago and have been worn away to their present size by the action of the elements. By comparison, the western mountains are young upstarts. None of them, not even the Rockies, is more than sixty million years old.

Putting such sectional rivalry aside, the mountains of this country, whether they be the old, worn ones of the East or the raw young ones of the West, provide people with a special kind of inspirational recreation. Three-fifths of the national parks include mountains among their primary attractions. From the Olympic National Park in Washington, with its snow-capped peaks and its lush rain forest, to the Rocky Mountain National Park in Colorado, which has sixty-five peaks more than 10,000 feet high, to the forest wonderland of the Great Smoky Mountains National Park, mountain environments have been set aside for the enjoyment of all the people.

When you ascend tall mountains, you pass through a series of life zones which otherwise could be visited only by traveling great distances. These zones are defined by the vegetation that predom-

138

inates at certain altitudes. In the Chiricahua Mountains, an iso-
lated range in Arizona, the Southwestern Research Station of the
American Museum of Natural History boasts that it can conduct
its visitors through five life zones in fifty minutes. The first of
these is the desert floor out of which the mountains rise. To the west
of the Chiricahuas lies the Sonoran Desert, to the east the Chihua-
huan, each with its traditional blend of grasses, cactus, and shrubs
evolved by the harsh conditions of sparse rainfall. Above, at ele-
vations of from about 4,000 to 5,500 feet, is the chaparral, a woodland belt named after the dwarf evergreen oak. Among the shrubs
and trees flourishing in this zone are algerita, manzanita lemon
bush, Apache plume, and service berry.

Higher up, the chaparral grades into the piñon-juniper cover.
This well-defined zone is marked by several species of juniper,
low-growing pine, scrub oak, spirea, mimosa, barberry, snake-
weed, rabbit brush, to name just a few. In general, it leaves off at
7,000 feet and gives way to the Douglas-fir/yellow-pine association,
which extends to the top of the mountains at a height of 9,795 feet.
Trees found in this zone are ponderosa pine, Engelmann spruce,
white fir, Douglas fir, and aspen.

Upon reaching the summit and finding himself in grassy glades
with iris, blue lupine, and columbine blooming around him, the
visitor can hardly believe that he left the sun-baked desert such a
short time before.

In north central Utah, they hold an annual hike which draws
enthusiasts from over most of the country. En masse, they ascend
to the summit of 12,000-foot Mount Timpanogos, highest peak of
the Wasatch Range. In climbing this mountain they make a trip
comparable to traveling from Utah to the Arctic Circle. Leaving
the typical western flora at the mountain's base, they follow trails
up through Engelmann spruce, white balsam, and alpine fir, and

Nighttime settles on exhausted hikers relaxing by campfire as sun's last rays light distant peaks. PHOTO BY TONI FRISSELL

Content with scaling 6,500 feet to perch on Mt. LeConte peak, tired climbers watch day's end. PHOTO BY RICHARD MEEK

then, to reach the top, they work their way up a glacier such as those found in the far North.

The Timp Hike, as it is called, was started in 1912 when Eugene Roberts, an instructor at Brigham Young University, led the first dozen hikers to the summit. Since then it has acquired a national reputation, and as many as 1,500 hikers have participated in a single assault on the mountain.

Although young as mountains go, the ranges of the West support the world's oldest known trees. First and foremost among these ancients are the giant sequoias that Americans have come to accept as part of their national heritage. The remaining groves, most of them safe in national parks and forests, have become botanical shrines. Millions of people have visited these titans on the western slope of the Sierra Nevada, but most of them are unaware that they came close to being destroyed.

In the Converse Basin, in what is now the Sequoia National Forest, there once stood one of the fine groves of *Sequoia gigantea*. It was logged off at the end of the last century and the basin today is dotted with great stumps, ten to twelve feet high and up to thirty feet in diameter. Solid cylinders of wood, they stand lifeless, but still defying destruction. At the edge of the basin, the lumbermen left one mighty specimen, called the Boole tree, which is 261 feet tall and thirty-five feet thick at its base. At a point 200 feet above the ground, it is ten feet thick. The Boole tree and many of the others in that grove were more than 3,000 years old.

It was the destruction of this grove that stirred public resentment and led to the preservation of most of the remaining stands. The Save the Redwoods League is still active. It now devotes its

144 efforts largely to buying and setting aside groves of the coastal

redwoods, another species which grows even taller, though not so bulky, as the giant sequoias.

The oldest sequoia scientifically dated was found to be 3,200 years old and was long regarded as earth's oldest living thing. But in the summers of 1954 and 1955, Dr. Edmund Schulman, of the University of Arizona, found some trees in the White Mountains, twenty miles northeast of Bishop, California, which were even older. These were gnarled bristlecone pines of unimpressive size which had grown in diameter at the rate of only a fraction more than an inch every hundred years! Dr. Schulman, by counting the growth rings, determined that three of these astonishingly persistent trees were more than 4,000 years old.

Mountains have served as natural sanctuaries for many species of animals, as well as trees. The mountain goat and the mountain sheep live in a high world of their own. The elk, the grizzly bear, and the mountain lion have flourished in mountainous country after being driven out of the lowlands by civilization. Here, they are the highly prized targets of the big-game hunters.

Like fishermen, hunters are divided into groups according to the species of their preference. There are those who relish the dangers of coping with an antagonized bear and others who prefer to exercise the skill involved in hunting the mountain sheep or mountain goat at high altitudes. The latter hunters dwell more upon the tortures of stalking their quarry among the rugged crags than they do upon the actual shooting. In a *Sports Illustrated* article, William A. Fisher, an ardent devotee of the sport, described its thrills as follows:

"In twelve years of hunting the majestic mountain sheep I have never met a man who does not admit to a sense of great excitement when at last he encounters this wild and elusive monarch   147

of America's high fastnesses. In part, it is the arduous nature of the hunt—the hours of climbing, waiting, climbing, usually in freezing cold; in part, the awe inspired by the remote wilderness in which he lives; but always, it is the regal, untamed vision of the sheep himself, his head erect with his great, curling horns, his forefeet planted on the crest of the world—a vision that can pull a man again and again through hardships inconceivable to anyone who has never experienced such visions."

Few persons attain the highest crags. The lower reaches of the mountains, however, supply unexpected thrills for the majority who go there for the pleasures of hiking and camping. The thrill of seeing a golden eagle soaring through mountain air is enough to make such a trip worth while.

Incidentally, in many respects the golden eagle is a more noble bird than our national symbol, the bald eagle. It took the founding fathers six years to decide on the national emblem and it was adopted only after considerable controversy; some espoused the golden eagle and Benjamin Franklin wanted the turkey gobbler. Despite their relative characteristics, the sight of either a golden or a bald eagle in flight is an inspiring thing to the mountain hiker.

Hiking is practiced by many, but most Americans have succumbed to the comfort of doing their sight-seeing from automobiles. These tourists are mainly families from urban centers who cruise along, soaking up the scenery, seldom leaving their cars except to have lunch by the roadside.

And the most mysterious trait of the great American tourist is his steadfast refusal to regard the bears in the national parks as wild animals. If a bear walked into a man's backyard, the householder would barricade himself inside in terror, phone the police, bawl out the mayor, and write an indignant letter to his Congress-   149 man. But let the same man and his family take to the highways of some national park and, like as not, they will ignore warnings, regulations, and fines, and go up and embrace the first bear they see, as though it were some long-lost relative.

This may seem to be an exaggeration, but it is not. The fascination that bears hold for the touring American public is a thing beyond understanding. Visitors to the national parks have done things to and with bears that would make a thoughtful man's hair curl. Take the ranger in the Great Smoky Mountains National Park who came upon this family scene: the man was holding his

Timp hikers duck behind cascade, one of nearly a hundred along route. PHOTO BY JOERN GERDTS

Sparkling in sunlight, North Carolina Cascades are treat for tourists. PHOTO BY EARL PALMER

small boy on the back of a full-grown black bear while his wife stood out front snapping pictures with carefree abandon. When the ranger drove the creature away with his three-foot bear stick and asked the man what in thunderation he thought he was doing, the man said the bears were tame and berated the ranger for spoiling the family's fun.

Most accidents result from feeding the bears. The tourist hands the bear half of his sandwich and then becomes terror-stricken when the bear advances to get the other half. If the tourist doesn't let go of his half real quick he is likely to have his arm ripped open. Many of these injuries are not reported because the victims know they were violating the law by getting chummy with a bear in the first place.

Many visitors to the parks spread their picnic lunches right on the shoulder of the highway. A bear comes along, frightens the picnickers back into their cars, and helps himself to one spread after another. Few of these people get sore at the bear. To have a bear eat your lunch is something to talk about when you get home. The bears are the greatest attraction in the Great Smoky Mountains National Park. Women have broken into tears when their visit ended without seeing a bear.

Motorists get into a frenzy when bears appear along the highway. Leaving their cars, they rush for the bear with food and cameras. Sometimes they forget to set their brakes and the car goes rolling down the mountainside. One time a Texan was driving through the park when his car was struck by another. He jumped out to raise sand, but was nonplused to find there was nobody in the other car. Its owner was somewhere up the mountain, concentrating on watching a bear.

152   Bears who leave their pursuit of natural foods to take up a life

of easy handouts along the highways soon associate automobiles with food. Many a car left open has been invaded. In a western national park, a man returned to his car to find a bear rummaging around in the back seat. The man stood by, wondering what to do. He watched as the bear climbed over into the front seat and continued its search for grub. The problem was solved when the bear sat down on the steering wheel and sounded the horn. The scared bear came out of the car, taking the front door with him. The man watched as the bear ran down the mountain with the car door draped around its neck.

Hunters write harrowing tales of experiences with bears, but the tourist likes to pet them. Once I was in the headquarters of the Great Smoky Mountains National Park when a group of girls in their early teens came in with a protest. Their leader was a young lady in shorts and pony tail who could not have been much older than her charges. They explained to the ranger on duty that they had obeyed all the rules and had kept their food locked in the car, but a bear came and tore the tent anyway.

They thought this was unfair of the bear and wanted to know if it would be all right if they threw rocks to chase him away. Trying to hide a smile, the ranger gave them permission to chase the bear. Quick investigation by another ranger disclosed that the critter in question was Fatso, a 600-pound male, who had become a troublemaker in his search for easy food.

The National Park Service would not think of getting rid of the bears because people love them so, but it dreams of the day when tourists will treat them as wild animals. It seems, though, that that day will never come. The tourist's yearning to get cozy with a wild bear remains the most mysterious trait of the species.

154   Bears certainly constitute a strong attraction, but they are

Touch of old west is preserved by Wyoming dude ranch where guests join evening roundups. PHOTO BY TONI FRISSELL

Montana's expanse of Bob Marshall Wilderness, named for farsighted conservationist who headed movement to preserve w eas, offers unequaled hunting to sportsmen willing to endure rigors of quarry's primitive habitat. PHOTO BY JOERN GERDTS

only one of many that bring people to the mountains. Mountain trout streams draw fishermen from afar. Nature lovers climb high to find rare plants or add new birds to their lists. There is one hardy group whose members devote their spare time to exploring the caves usually found in mountainous regions. The study and exploration of caves is called speleology and those who practice it call themselves spelunkers. Their hobby is mountain climbing in reverse and, like mountain climbers, they use ropes, axes, and other equipment to facilitate their underground expeditions.

Their numbers are meager, however, when compared to the swarms of skiers who take to the mountains as soon as the snow begins to fly. In recent years skiing has done more to get the American people back on their feet than any other outdoor sport. Its growth has been phenomenal. A generation ago there were two classes of skiers in this country. One was a small group of specialists and professionals who awed spectators with their daring leaps. The other was made up of kids sliding down hills with barrel staves on their feet. Since then their numbers have mushroomed and millions of dollars have been spent to provide facilities for a new type of outdoorsman who is happiest when he is sliding down snow-covered slopes. New resorts appear each year; Colorado alone boasts twenty ski centers.

As late as 1930, the village of Stowe, Vermont, was still unaware of the fact that if good facilities were provided, thousands of enthusiastic skiers would come and spend lots of money pursuing their sport. Sun Valley, Idaho, which is known throughout the country even to people who have never seen snow, did not have its first season until 1937. Improved equipment and the advent of ski tows which took the drudgery out of skiing were important in the increase of the sport's popularity. Now the skiing fraternity

Inspiring to mountain hikers is sight of great golden eagle soaring in flight. Here ready to land on studio perch, magnificent eagle braces tail and wings, spreads talons and flight plumes, maneuvers for position. Bird gets braking power from seven-foot wingspread and powerful pectoral muscles. PHOTO BY DAVID GOODNOW

Warmly clad sightseers and pet poodle prepare for invigorating sleighride through Colorado highlands. PHOTO BY RICHARD MEF

"Suicide Six," site of Dartmouth College ski events near Woodstock, Vermont, was painted by Byron Thomas.

*Exhilarating mile-long ride in chair lift up
mountain at Stowe, Vermont, is almost as much fun as
swift slide down. Halfway up, skiers switch
to T-bar to complete trip.* PHOTO BY JERRY COOKE

can spend more time on the downgrade. Weekend skiers and those who can get out only for one day hurry over to the ski tow at the end of each run to squeeze as much time on the slopes as they possibly can.

Great impetus also was given to skiing when resorts began to make it a family sport. In the early days a young couple bent on a skiing holiday would park the offspring with relatives. Now the whole family goes along to resorts equipped to handle visitors of all ages. New England establishments, in particular, have a variety of services which attract families. Some resorts have baby sitters for infants and a nursery where the three- to five-year-olds can be corraled while the older members of the family are out on the slopes. There are special instructors for children from six to nine years. There are J-bar lifts, easy for children to ride, and many novice slopes are in full view from the windows of the lodge.

Mount Snow, in Vermont, has six double-chair lifts, including a baby-chair lift only 700 feet long for rank beginners and another one 2,000 feet long for novices. It also has a heated, outdoor swimming pool surrounded by a sun deck and glass walls, the first of its kind in the East.

At Snow Ridge, New York, the staff watches toddlers while parents ski and cribs are provided free of charge. At Catamount, New York, they have a slope where offspring too small to ski slide down in flying saucers. There usually is a room where the kids can play games, read books, or otherwise amuse themselves. Most places offer reduced rates on everything for children.

Each year several million skiers hie themselves to one or another of the country's 250 ski areas. Regularly, winter trains set out from Boston, New York, Chicago, and Detroit. Even Californians forsake the palm trees to take the Union Pacific's Snow-

166

Swooping through pelting winds and glaring sun on wide trails at Stowe, is endless thrill for both expert and weekend snow bunny.

ball Limited to Sun Valley. The airlines carry skiers in search of new slopes on which to slide: easterners going to the West and the Rockies, Chicagoans to Vermont and the Green Mountains, Texans to Utah's Wasatch Range.

Above the realm of the skier lies the grim, spectacular upper world of snow and rock and rarefied air that is the domain of the mountain climber. Probably few sports are more specialized or have fewer practitioners in their ranks, or a larger army of armchair enthusiasts. Ever since the sixteenth century, when a party of Cortez' soldiers climbed the sacred volcano, Mount Popocatepetl, in search of saltpeter, the mystical challenge of ascending to a mountain's peak has gripped the imagination of men.

One by one, with the passage of time, the great towers have been conquered, but such are the unique hazards of the assault that even in defeat there is no dishonor. And whether because climbers are unusually articulate men or because the fever of the

168

quest makes them kin with poets, it is fact that no sport (except, possibly, skin diving) has been so rapturously, so beautifully, so profoundly reported.

Climbing hazardous heights is usually done only by the most experienced alpinists. In one instance, however, two men with virtually no previous experience at mountain climbing reached the summit of Mount McKinley, North America's highest peak, which rises 20,320 feet. The two were Woodrow Wilson Sayre, a grandson of President Woodrow Wilson, and Norman Hansen, a Boston lawyer. In order to get permission to climb the mountain, they teamed up with three U.C.L.A. students, Jac Lasner, Norman Sanders, and Jon Gardi, who had mountaineering experience. Sayre and Hanson were short on experience but had read a lot of books on mountain climbing.

Sayre's story about the climb in *Sports Illustrated* was a lesson to all who dream of climbing mountains without the years of 169

In breath-taking moment of perfect control, jumper seems suspended in sky above Oregon's Mt. Hood. PHOTO BY RAY ATKESON

*Combining thrills of two worlds, Sun Valley
visitors (left) take relaxing plunge in steam-heated
pools after day of skiing mountain trails.*

*Incongruous sight in valley are bathers (below)
trotting across snow-blanketed hillsides and
burying themselves in white drifts while hot Idaho
sun beats down.* PHOTOS BY JOERN GERDTS

gruelling preparation. After describing the major part of the ascent, he wrote:

"The next day was sunny. We dried out and moved up against a strong headwind to 16,000 feet. The weather looked so good we decided to try for the summit in one push. It felt fine to be without packs, but the altitude was troublesome. The morning's headache hung on and I had to take one to four breaths each step. Finally, at about 19,000 feet, I felt that I had passed my limit, and Norm and I turned back. We returned to camp and four hours later the others straggled in. They had made it but were so tired they couldn't eat until the next afternoon. Jon's returning words were: 'Well, you couldn't ever pay me enough to do that again!'

"Meanwhile, Norm and I were resigned to our 'good try.' But as we got rested, we were gradually able to think of another effort, if the weather held. And it did hold.

"That night at Denali Pass the wind dropped and we grew excited, feeling that we might have a chance after all. The summit above us turned to deep gold against the obsidian-blue backdrop of a high-altitude sky. And the following day was calm and clear.

"We made our try, and it was a sign of how worn we were that it took us ten hours to climb the 2,120 feet to the top that day. But at last we stood there. We were too tired to feel any great thrill. But there was gratitude for such a wonderful day and for being there at all. We photographed frantically in all directions. After fifteen minutes we started down.

"The expedition's descent took four days. Tempers wore thin. We noticed that we were all barking at each other quite regularly. Still, I don't think we realized how long-term weary we were. At home, I found I had lost fifteen pounds. Food seemed rather taste-

174 less and I seemed to notice far fewer sights and sounds. I felt as if

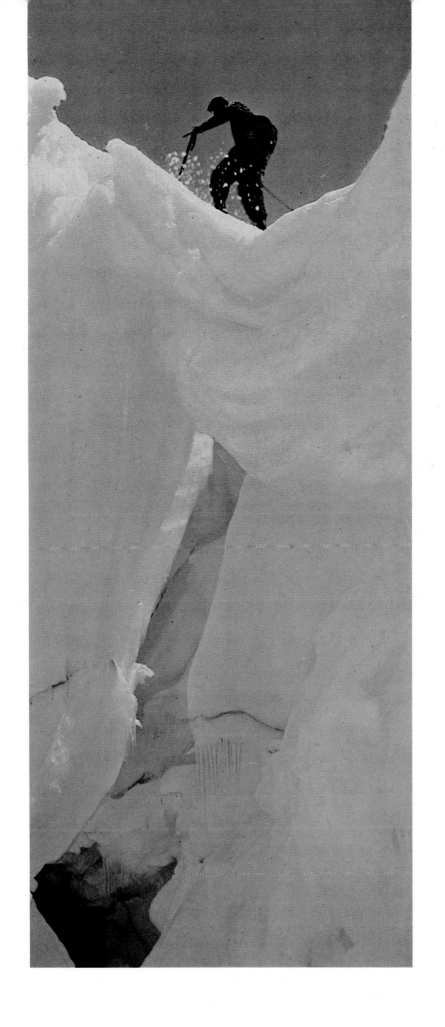

Successful ascent puts mountaineer astride the world. Here climber pauses to enjoy panorama from summit of Alaska's Mt. McKinley, highest North American peak. PHOTO BY NORMAN HANSEN

I were under water. I noticed that I rarely whistled or sang. Most of the symptoms left in a fortnight. But the dead spots on my fingers and toes and the glacier burns on my lips lasted over a month.

"Was our lack of experience a real handicap? On this particular trip, thanks to great good fortune, I do not think it was. But if various emergencies had risen, needing a sure technique of ice ax or rope handling, the story might have been a different one.

"Certainly, there is a lot of fetish in mountain climbing, as there is in any specialty, and a lot of sacred cows which could well be shot and eaten. But, if the nonexpert is planning to beard the expert in his den he should be always aware that the odds are against him. On Mount McKinley they are even more against him now than when I was there. The Park Rangers, for example, are more stringent in passing climbing parties. And Muldrow Glacier, which we found so smooth, is now twisted into a jumble of ice ... and it is a major alpine feat just to cross it.

"Thus I proved my point—but I discovered two things that for four years since I have been drumming into various hopefuls who have heard about my climb and want to try something like it. First, there is no comforting substitute for experience. Second, luck is the indispensable factor in success by the inexperienced. The most important piece of equipment I had with me on Mount McKinley, along with my book learning, was a genuine, guaranteed, pretested and foolproof rabbit's foot."

For most of us, even a rabbit's foot would be no inducement to climb the breath-taking heights. Nor is it necessary that we do so, for love of the mountains comes as easily from friendly proximity and admiration as from conquest. From the peak, after all, one can no longer see the mountain.   179

*The elemental water is home
and haven to angler as well as
fish, to diving boy, to
long canoe and silent sail, and
to the idle dreamer ashore*

LAKES

STREAMS

The lakes and streams of America attract more people in search of recreation than any other outdoor scene. You might not think so, judging by the hordes of people you encounter every time you visit an ocean beach, but just imagine what is going on at the same time throughout the inland realm of fresh water. The millions of fishermen, the families picnicking on the river banks, the sailboats fluttering over the lakes like hatches of mayflies; kids in countless swimming holes, outboards droning like beetles, and swarms of small fry at lakeside summer camps—altogether they become a mighty panorama.

What is this great attraction that water has for people? Scientists say that because man originally emerged from the water, he likes to return to it, to indulge a primordial urge to immerse himself in the stuff whence he came. There may be something in this theory, but I think there is a lot more to the phenomenon than that. I'm willing to bet that even if all our ancestors had come from Kansas, we would still find all our senses responding strongly to water.

Water is inanimate, a blending of basic elements into a colorless liquid, yet the lakes and streams composed of it are living things. This is true because the very presence of water causes life   183

*Skimming over glassy lake in Manitoba's
watery wilderness, pike fishermen search for long,
ugly fish which natives scornfully
call "snake."* PHOTO BY ERWIN A. BAUER

to flourish. There is life in the water. If a pond is green or brown, it is because of the myriad of tiny things abiding there. There is life along the banks and life in the air above. There is also motion. It is because of this combination that each lake, river, creek, or brook has character, and because it has character it has moods.

Think of a rattling mountain brook. It is all vibrance, alive and in a hurry, always in the same place, but different each time you visit it. The poets speak of it as "the laughing brook." I don't know whether it is laughing or not, but the sight of it makes *me* laugh in sheer delight. Think of a small midwestern river winding 185

Fly casting, like putting or the three-cushion carom, is skill that adds cubits to a man's stature, although one need not be expert to enjoy sport thoroughly. PHOTO BY JERRY COOKE

Famous quarry of fresh-water fishermen across nation, agile rainbow trout are usually found in cold, white water. PHOTO BY MARTIN IGER

186

Wily trout abound in lovely western rivers, like Snake, in hundred-mile circle of Yellowstone National Park area. Fly fishermen must be skilled to catch them. PHOTO BY ROBERT HOLLAND

lazily through the still heat of summer. Just to sit in the shade of a tree and watch the quiet flow gives you something that no tadpole emerging from the cosmic ooze could ever have felt. Take the farm pond in the meadow or the brown tide of the Mississippi carrying the waters of a thousand lesser streams—each pulses with life and brings deep emotions to all those who love it.

Just listen to a group of trout fishermen discussing their favorite stream. Under their searching appraisal, it is manifest that the watercourse of which they speak is a cherished friend whose bad moods are to be tolerated and whose genial ones are to be shared. The stream is too high or too low, muddy or clear. Seldom is it just right and that is all for the best. If it were just right all the time there would be little for the fishermen to talk about and nothing on which their fishless days could be blamed.

Fishermen are divided into as many tribes as there are types of streams and lakes. Each has its traditional rites and beliefs. The fly-fishing tribe is the most ritualistic of all, regarding its activity more as an art form than as a sport. To hear the tribesmen talk, they consider tradition and method more important than the actual taking of fish, although I've never met one who kept silent after landing a whopper. Some of them are so horrified at the thought of anyone using worms for bait that they refuse to speak the name of the squirmy critter, referring to it with downright loathing as "barnyard hackle."

Even within the tribe there are continuing controversies, usually concerning the merits of the various species of trout. There are grizzled sachems of long experience who hold that the imported brown trout, the first significant shipment of which came to this country in egg form from Germany in 1883, is to be preferred above all other species. They contend that, because it is the hardest to catch, it provides the supreme test of skill for the purist, the man who scorns any lure but dry flies.

There are others who espouse the rainbow or the eastern brook trout just as insistently, and among northwestern fishermen are those who feel that to enter icy streams in the dead of winter to fish   189

Gluttonous chain pickerel gets hooked
on artificial lure. Pickerel is plucky fighter found
in shallow, weedy waters east of Appalachians from
Canada to Florida, and in Mississippi Valley.

Largemouth black bass is taken by anglers from southern Canada to northeastern Mexico, prefers waters with mud bottom. It is now stocked in many small farm ponds. PHOTOS BY MARTIN IGER

*Perched on rock above roaring, treacherous Colorado
River, veteran riverwoman Georgie White watches as two of her
boats shoot Horn Rapids. Complete Grand Canyon run
is over 300 miles long.* PHOTO BY RICHARD A. SMITH

for steelhead is comparable only to passing through the pearly gates of heaven. Outside the trout-fishing clan are those who hold the smallmouthed bass to be the superlative fish. They have to admit that the largemouth runs bigger, but they insist that "pound for pound the smallmouthed bass is the gamest fish that swims." There are smaller groups whose members worship the muskellunge, extol the northern pike, or even revere the chain pickerel.

Once I was standing in the yard of a motel in South Carolina when a boy of the ten-year-old variety came up to me and, without the formality of an introduction, announced, "Me and Grandpaw are goin' fishin'." He wore a wide grin and his anticipation was so great he could hardly keep still. Subsequent conversation disclosed that the objective of the expedition was to catch sunfish.

That, despite the praise lavished on larger species, is the objective of most American fishing trips. The family of small, freshwater sunfishes, whose wide variety of names includes sunny, punkinseed, redbreast, bluegill, bream, and stump knocker, represents the majority of fish caught in American lakes and streams.

These colorful panfish are so prolific that, if nothing happened to the eggs or young of a single pair, the descendants would number in the millions within a few years. But plenty does happen to them. The young are the food of many predators, including the bass. Small boys and their grandfathers, as well as a host of fishermen in between, should raise some sort of a monument to the prolific sunny. It is found over most of the country and is usually the first fish—and often the last—that a man catches.

Finally, there is the all-purpose fisherman, the member of no tribe, the type that glows at the mere mention of the sport, who will settle for practically any kind of catch and who gets a big kick out of every aspect of a fishing trip. My Uncle Jim was a prime

Dense thicket of lines and masts jams Chicago pier as racing fleet gets set for 333-mile dash over Lake Huron to Mackinac Island. Fifty or more of Midwest's crack skippers participate in this annual classic. PHOTO BY DAVID KITZ

example of the all-purpose fisherman. A city man, Uncle Jim
spent much of his spare time—and a great deal he couldn't spare—
in planning and dreaming of his excursions for fish.

Oddly enough, his very eagerness made him a poor fisherman,
as far as technique was concerned. He was always trying new
gadgets, only a few of which ever worked. No matter how long he
pored over his tackle, something awful usually happened at the
crucial moment. Something was *always* happening to him. A porcupine would chew the handle off his canoe paddle. His boat would
spring a leak. Once he cast over a limb of a tree and hooked a bass.
He lost the bass and in climbing the tree to retrieve his lure he tore
his pants. Uncle Jim was always tearing his pants.

Another time, he was on a Wisconsin lake, two miles from
shore, when a sudden storm came up. High wind, black clouds, and
thunder threatened as he tried frantically to get his early model
outboard motor started. He twisted the starting knob so hard that
it came off and dropped to the bottom of the lake. Uncle Jim had
no alternative but to row for his life, swearing as he rowed. I've
seen him sitting in a boat at dusk with mosquitoes around him in a
whining cloud. Did he give up for the day? Not Uncle Jim! He put
on his headnet, rolled down his sleeves, and continued to cast while
the mosquitoes bit his bare wrists unmercifully.

He was a ghastly sight when he returned from one of these
pleasure trips. His face was drawn. His whole body exuded
fatigue. His gear was a mess and the hole in his pants was only
partially closed with a safety pin. But his eyes were bright, his
enthusiasm undimmed. As long as he could stay awake he would
sit and tell about the wonderful things that had happened, of the
big ones he had caught and the bigger ones he had lost. The bad
things were omitted or joked about, and before he put his weary

frame to bed there was always the report of the wonderful new spot some fellow had told him about where the fish would jump into the boat to get at your lure. He never found that fisherman's Utopia, but he searched for it as long as he lived. I'm not sure he would have been happy to find it.

Uncle Jim may have been an extreme case, but there is some of his ardor in every fisherman. It is impossible to learn how many fishermen there are because not all of them are required to have a license. A recent report, however, estimated the number at thirty million. Whatever the total, it is growing at least as rapidly as our exploding population, and fishermen are putting ever-mounting pressure on the places to fish.

The uncontrollable urge to catch fish causes some anglers to do strange things. In some regions, where fishing places are scarce,

the eager ones follow the fish-hatchery truck. Word spreads that the truck is on the way to a lake and a long line of cars falls in behind it. The live cargo is dumped into the lake. The anglers line up, shoulder to shoulder, and fish until the lake is depleted. Then, with heavy creels, they all go away to await the next stocking.

Some sort of record was established at Crowley Lake, in California, on the opening day of the 1957 trout season when 10,030 anglers in 3,178 boats took out eighteen-and-a-half tons of stocked trout. Traditionalists frown upon such frantic fishing, claiming that the hatchery truck followers are missing most of the fun in their eagerness to make a big catch. I know one æsthete who toils over the boulders of a small stream, usually catches one or two measly trout, returns home and sits down to a big roast beef, which his intelligent wife has prepared. He never expects to catch many

201

Flotilla of gaily decorated sailboats and motor cruisers parades through canal on way to Union Bay in Seattle. Spring procession officially opens city's boating season.
PHOTO BY BURT GLINN

Powerboat chugs leisurely up uninhabited section of narrow northern waterway where clear waters provide relaxing swimming and glacier-polished rocks are perfect for sunbathing. PHOTO BY DAVID KITZ

fish, but when he fails to catch any, he can't hide his gloom.

Science, of course, is bringing new hope to fishermen through a drastic revolution in the management of fishing waters. There was a time when the fish and game departments of the various states operated on the theory that all they had to do to maintain good fishing was to limit the size and number of fish taken. This practice had been in force for years and was firmly implanted in the public mind before biologists began intensive research in fish management.

During these experiments they made some astonishing discoveries. Generally, they established that over-fishing was not the cause of bad fishing. They learned that some species multiply so fast they become too numerous for the available food. The evidence suggested that better fishing would result if more fish were taken; the more you took, the faster the remaining ones would grow because they would get a larger share of the food. This called

for an immediate about-face in fish management.

It was difficult to achieve, however, because both the fishermen and the administrators had long been operating on the opposite theory. But gradually more and more states began to do away with closed seasons and, in some cases, size limits. At the same time, they concentrated their efforts on better management and stream improvement. Basic research on the problem of better fishing is going on in most states. Meanwhile, the nation's fishermen are not just looking forward to better fishing; they are spending their money for it and demanding results. The total sale of fishing and hunting licenses in the United States in 1958 amounted to $99,018,130. Minnesota, California, Wisconsin, and Michigan, each sold more than a million fishing licenses.

America is blessed not only with hundreds of thousands of small streams and ponds which are the fishermen's delight, but with larger ones adaptable to the various forms of pleasure boat-

Life along Boston's Charles River becomes cheerfully casual under warming influence of June sun. Riverbank loungers, indolent angler, and four-oared shell passing Harvard's Dunster House are New England taking its ease. PHOTOS BY FARRELL GREHAN

ing. Here, again, Americans are a lucky people, for the postwar boating boom has vastly increased the requirement for water on which to float this new-found enthusiasm. At the same time, the perfection of the boat trailer now enables the city man to keep a boat in his yard or garage, and haul it out onto the highways whenever he must travel a distance to find water.

The boating mania that has gripped a large part of the populace takes many forms, some of them positively odd. While driving along one day, I came upon a pretty little pond that couldn't have

been more than 150 feet in diameter. There was nothing unusual
about the pond itself—the countryside is dotted with farm ponds—
but this one sported a twenty-foot motor cruiser. A man had backed
his trailer up to the bank and launched the craft. There he was,
chugging around in a tight circle. He wasn't going anywhere, but
he seemed happy because he kept waving gaily to a woman who
stood on shore, undoubtedly an adoring wife.

And how about those wild-water addicts who go out to Arizona and shoot the rapids of the Colorado as it tumbles through

Silhouetted against coppery lake at sunset, youthful paddlers head back to camp after race. Symbolic of end of active summer day for millions of youngsters, glowing lake at nightfall will reflect colors of campfires lit along shore. PHOTO BY TONI FRISSELL

the Grand Canyon? Professional rapid shooters do a good business taking customers on this perilous trip. Among them is Georgie White, a veteran riverwoman, who supervises a fleet of inflated rafts which make the trip with paying guests.

My friend, Joel Sayre, made the Grand Canyon run in one of her boats and hasn't been the same since. The mere sight of the rapids scared the liver out of him; his boat upset and he got wetter than he ever had been in his whole life. But when it was all over he was a convert. In writing about the trip, he said:

"In my opinion the Almighty laid out the Grand Canyon run with absolute perfection of design. Every now and then there is something ineffably exciting and exhilarating to attack, but in between come stretches of peace in which you recover from the exhilaration and excitement.

"The Colorado is a very complex body of water, complex in the way that a powerful human personality is. I have spoken of it as that damned Colorado, but many times I have truly thought of it as blessed. There is its rapacious, treacherous, merciless, uninhibited side—the one you always read and hear about; but it also has a side that can be beneficial and moving. To sleep on the bank of the Colorado is a splendid thing: a man derives a replenishing inner sustenance from the earth, and from the river, too."

Shooting the scary rapids of the Colorado or paddling a canoe on a placid pond both have their attractions, but there are many other reasons why so many citizens have become water-borne. Boat and engine manufacturers design their products to fit any pocketbook or preference. In 1948, for example, Alex Bryan, who made iceboats and surfboards in Waterbury, Connecticut, experimented by attaching a fin and a rudder to one of his surfboards. Mounting an old canoe sail on the contraption, he sailed around. That was the beginning of the Sailfish, the quick, colorful little craft that now brightens thousands of American lakes.

212

Lakeside at Camp Sunapee, New Hampshire, typifies
summer camp scenes across nation where well-watered
boys seem to grow several inches under
beneficent rays of sun. PHOTO BY TONI FRISSELL

The advantages of the Sailfish are that it is about the cheapest sailing craft on the market. It can be stored in the cellar and hauled around on top of a station wagon. And it is unsinkable. Finally, it can give a family as much sailing fun as a boat many times its size. Sailing a Sailfish is a wet and hilarious pastime.

To get a clear picture of just how boat-conscious this country is, pop around to some of the dozens of big boating centers during the height of the season. Drop in at Chicago's lake front to see fifty or more yachts in the spectacular start of the 333-mile race to Mackinac Island. The Mackinac, billed as the longest fresh-water sailing event in the world, draws the finest skippers of the Midwest. After the race the yachtsmen hold a succession of parties aboard their boats and ashore on rustic Mackinac Island, where automobiles are forbidden and visitors ride from the dockside on bicycles and in horse-drawn carriages.

Or go out to Lake Geneva, Wisconsin, during the latter part of the summer when the Class A scows are staging their championships and you will see some of the world's most frantic racing. Class A scows are thirty-eight foot sloops whose flat-bottomed design, with twin rudders and twin bilge boards, gives them speeds up to thirty-five miles per hour. Scows are built for racing and come in classes ranging down to little eighteen-footers.

Anybody used to thinking of Detroit in terms of automobiles gets a stunning surprise when he drops in on the city's waterfront on any pleasant weekend. Here he finds one of the greatest hotbeds of boating in the whole country. The Detroit Yacht Club, with its 3,300 members and 384 berths, is the biggest yacht club in the world, and it is only one of half a dozen big clubs of which the city   215

boasts. Among them is the Detroit Boating Club, established in
1839, which claims to be the oldest boating association in the
United States. Among its many activities, it supports a program
in the old-fashioned sport of rowing.

In the line of powered boats, Detroit puts everything into the
water from roaring hydroplanes to pint-sized outboards. Put them
all together—the hydro men with their speedy monsters, the out-
216 boarders with their trailers, and the sailors with their pretty

Shady banks of Scioto River attract Columbus, Ohio families on Sunday afternoons in summer to picnic and watch hydroplanes perform in noisy, colorful regatta. PHOTO BY RICHARD MEEK

sloops and yawls—and you get one of the most variegated scenes of boating activity anywhere in the world.

Jump out to Seattle and you find the scene repeated on almost as large a scale. Seattle has the advantage of both fresh and salt-water boating right at the city's doorstep. Beautiful Lake Washington lies in town, and to reach the wonderful cruising waters of Puget Sound the boaters have only to pass through a lock.

Once on a summer weekend a friend invited me for a Sunday cruise on Lake Washington. In the late afternoon we reached the two parallel locks that form the gateway between lake and sound. Here hundreds of boats were returning from weekend salt-water cruises. Both locks were operating at the same time, lifting squadron after squadron of pleasure boats back into their home lake. The lower gates of the biggest lock would open and two dozen or more assorted craft would crowd into it. After they had been lifted to the lake level, the upper gates would open and the flotilla would push on. Immediately, the water dropped in the lock so another gang of boats could be lifted. This went on and on. Watching the performance, one would think Americans were just naturally amphibious people.

When the herpetologists speak of amphibians they mean that group of animals—including toads and frogs—which spends part of its life in water and part on land. In my opinion, the group should be broadened to include small boys. I won't mind if they let small girls in, too, but generally speaking, small boys are more at home in the water than their sisters.

The sheer animal ecstasy of a bunch of boys swimming is a wonderful thing to behold. When the boy grows into a man he may still like to go swimming, but the screaming delight that he once knew has been left behind with his youth. James Whitcomb Riley

220

Ship's crew (at left) fights to control hull of world champion Class-A iceboat about to take flight. Skeeter class boats (below) vie for position on frosty speedway at 100 mph. PHOTOS BY ED STEIN

expressed this loss in "The Old Swimmin'-Hole." In case you don't remember, he had this to say in the last verse:

Oh! the old swimmin'-hole! When I last saw the place,
The scenes was all changed, like the change in my face;
The bridge of the railroad now crosses the spot
Whare the old divin'-log lays sunk and fergot.
And I stray down the banks whare the trees ust ter be—
But never again will theyr shade shelter me!
And I wish in my sorrow I could strip to the soul,
And dive off in my grave like the old swimmin'-hole.

More and more, old swimmin'-holes are being swallowed up as American cities spread out into vast urban complexes. This same growth of the urban areas, however, has given rise to another American tradition—the summer camp for youngsters.

Sending a boy off to his first summer camp means that the lad is getting out from under his mother's wing. There are the tears the mother tries to hide and the childish trepidation as the adventurer sets out into his new world of canoes and lakes, campfires in the wilderness, swimming, fishing, and hiking. It is also a world of eerie night sounds and the sudden, gnawing yen for home.

And when winter comes, not all the northern ponds, lakes, and streams are abandoned. Some outdoorsmen consider that a brook gurgling under snow, flowing beneath cliffs draped with icicles and glinting in winter sunshine, is prettier than at any other time of the year. Fishermen cannot be stopped by cold weather, a fact proved by the frozen lakes dotted with fishing shanties.

And don't forget the old skating pond. In my section there is an old canal where conditions sometimes are just right: smooth, thick ice without a covering of snow. When these conditions occur, young and old turn out with their skates and glide along the canal for several miles in grand style.

From the first trout fisherman of spring to the last skater of winter, the lakes and streams of America are providing the finest type of recreation for millions of people. It is up to those millions to make sure that these outdoor treasures don't go the way of Riley's old swimmin'-hole.

Frosty fire prolongs skaters' fun on woodland pond in Maine. PHOTO BY KOSTI RUOHOMAA

PLAINS &

Westward the country grows great. The expanse of green waving grain gives way to illimitable prairie and then to parched and sunburned sand

DESERT

Desert riders build big appetites during pre-breakfast jaunt. Party heads across Smoke Tree Flat, near Palm Springs, toward mountains and San Andreas Canyon. PHOTO BY JOHN BRYSON

At nightfall the desert comes to life. As dusk spreads across the land the animals emerge from their hiding places. By the time the moon takes over the duties of the sun, the desert is a busy place. Kangaroo rats skip daintily on their long hind legs; skunks prowl for insects; pack rats search for useless objects to add to their storage piles; snakes hunt rats and mice; coyotes howl on moonlit crests; rabbits frisk warily, always alert to the approach of bobcat or mountain lion. On a night when the moon is full, more wildlife can be seen in the desert than in any wooded area.

By day the desert seems comparatively lifeless. The sun's rays descend upon the land through an atmosphere seldom blurred by clouds, haze, or smog. Upon striking the bare rocks and sand they are reflected to produce a burning heat in which few of the desert animals could survive long exposure. Even a rattlesnake, forced

228

to remain in this relentless sunshine, would die in a short time.

In this superheated landscape the desert plants stand in an array of bizarre shapes. Cactuses, ranging from giant saguaros forty feet tall to pincushions that lie on the ground like small, thorny stones, have learned to thrive where less rugged plants would shrivel. Their impervious hides keep the moisture stored in their pulpy insides and their sharp spines give protection against animals that would eat them. Scraggly bushes and trees, many sporting thorns, send root systems deep into the soil for water.

All these plants and animals have adjusted themselves to the harsh conditions of sparse rainfall and intense heat, adaptations evolved over thousands of years. In prehistoric times, man did not fare so well in the American deserts. Archaeological evidence shows that during times of extreme drought, ancient peoples were driven   229

Strolling over New Mexico's undulating White Sands, three youthful vacationers emphasize the vastness of desert sprawling in serene splendor under purple San Andreas Mountain Range. PHOTO BY HORACE BRISTOL

out to seek more hospitable climates. The Salton Sea, in southern California, filled and dried up several times as the result of changes in the course of the Colorado River. Scientists have established that thousands of people once lived around the sea, only to disappear when it was reclaimed by the desert.

Now the American deserts are undergoing another human invasion. But this time there is a vast difference. Man, like the plants and animals, has learned how to be comfortable while living in this arid environment. To supply himself with water he drills wells to tap ancient reservoirs deep within the earth. To cool himself during the heat of the day, he resorts to air conditioning, and when shadows lengthen, he emerges like the kangaroo rat and the rabbit to enjoy himself in the cool of the evening.

Tourists used to drive across deserts to see their stark beauty but they seldom thought of staying there. In this modern invasion thousands spend their vacations at desert resorts. They play on desert golf courses, ride horseback over desert trails, and swim in the pools which are a part of these modern oases. Ghost towns which lost their means of support when the mines failed are coming to life again as tourist attractions. National parks and national monuments in desert and semi-desert country are hard put to handle the flow of people who are discovering that the sandy plains are as pleasant for vacationing as the sandy seashore.

The invasion forces are not made up entirely of vacationing tourists—far from it. Southwestern cities surrounded by cactus-studded land are spreading out into desert suburbs. Families are going right out into the harshest desert to build winter or year-round homes. Architects are having a field day designing houses which provide comfort yet fit tastefully into the rocky landscape. Tucson, Arizona, is a perfect example. This old city is growing at a phenomenal rate, with modern homes pushing out into territory once thought suitable only for Gila monsters and jack rabbits.

Those who have not seen this march of modernism into the desert have a surprise in store for them, and old timers who have watched it still can hardly believe what they see. The new crop of

Charging like Indians, Santa Fe horsemen practice palmetto polo. PHOTO BY JERRY COOKE

desert addicts seeks out the roughest locations for their homes; the more cactus on the plot the better. Houses are constructed without disturbing this natural growth, so that every yard is a cactus garden. After their completion the owners and their guests swim in the pool during the heat of the day, dine and lounge on the terrace in the evening. There they sit, looking out over a backyard studded with towering saguaros, huge barrel cactus, weird-shaped chollas, and prickly pear.

These new desert dwellers pass much of their spare time investigating the countryside around them, learning its history, taking in its colorful scenery, and watching its wildlife. They find that the best place to learn about the desert is at the Arizona-Sonora Desert Museum, fifteen miles from Tucson. Located in Tucson Mountain Park, in the midst of a forest of giant saguaros, this institution is not a museum in the accepted sense, but a combina- 233

tion of museum, zoo, and botanical garden.

The Desert Museum came into being as the result of a chance meeting between two men. One was Arthur N. Pack, philanthropist and conservationist, who, with his father, the late Charles Lathrop Pack, had started the American Tree Association and the Pack Forestry Foundation. The other was William H. Carr, a genius at interpreting nature by means of visual exhibits, who had built the Trailside Museum, at Bear Mountain, New York. Pack supplied the money, Carr supplied the design, and the Desert Museum was opened to the public in 1952. Its visitors, numbering more than 200,000 a year, include travelers from all over the country. They see live animals native to Arizona and the adjacent state of Sonora, Mexico, and they see the plant life of the same region growing in natural profusion.

At this institution everybody gets into the act and is encouraged to do so wherever feasible. Visitors are always delighted to read such signs as the one over the collection of mineral specimens which says, "If you are interested, please handle." Local interest is so great that the museum has had to buy only three animals: two mountain lions and a jaguar. All the rest were donated by enthusiastic citizens who came toting everything from horned toads to wildcats.

One afternoon a helicopter landed right on the museum grounds and a couple of grinning GIs got out and handed over to museum officials a box containing three fine, diamondback rattlesnakes. Earlier, the museum had loaned the Corps of Engineers at Fort Huachuca some animals to use in their desert survival course. The engineers were repaying the favor.

Easterners who go there with a preconceived idea that the desert is a dreary, lifeless place soon change their minds when   235 they see displays interpreting the relationships of the plants and animals in this stark environment. One popular exhibit delineates the life history of the saguaro cactus.

As they approach the museum, visitors are impressed by the thousands of giants of the cactus world that stand in the valleys and march up the mountainsides. Although austere plants of simple form, each saguaro has its own personality. Some raise thorn-studded arms in supplication. Some seem to beckon. Some, standing side by side with curving arms held aloft, appear to be engaged in some sort of cactus communication. Others assume comical poses and some appear dejected.

In the museum exhibit, the growth of saguaros is demonstrated with living specimens. The manner in which they store water inside their heavy trunks is explained, and by pulling a handle visitors can raise a trap-door to expose the roots of one large specimen. They learn how the Gila woodpecker digs its nesting holes in the saguaros and how twelve other species of birds come along and nest in the old woodpecker holes.

The life and times of the saguaro is but one of the desert stories told at the museum. Visitors always want to know what becomes of the desert animals in the daytime. To answer this oft-repeated question an elaborate tunnel has been constructed. Visitors go underground and peer through windows to see badgers, snakes, kit foxes, and other desert creatures curled up in their burrows. Through glass panels they see huge root systems, and by looking into a periscope they see the plants that own the roots growing in the sunshine above. There is even a cave with live bats hanging on its walls.

As the invasion of the desert gains momentum, the water problem becomes more acute. Wells supplying water for household

236

*Cattle ranching inspired growing sport of
cutting and holding cattle from herd. Among top
performers are Quarter Horses. Some of them
can do the job without rider.* PHOTO BY HY PESKIN

use, for swimming pools and agriculture, are diminishing underground supplies which took centuries to build up. To impress upon its visitors the critical nature of this problem, the Desert Museum recently added an impressive display of devices and instruments to tell the story of water, its proper use, and its relation to the soil and to man. There is no other exhibit like it, and after seeing it the modern desert dweller has more respect for his swimming pool.

When not enjoying the desert itself, newcomers become spectators or participants in sports that are traditional in the West. The rodeo, of course, has become a big-time sport, with professionals following the circuit of the larger shows. Another offshoot of the cattle industry is the sport of cutting. In this contest a man on horseback has to cut a calf out from a herd and move it to a given spot. The contestant who cuts out a given number of calves in the least time wins. Success in this sport depends largely on a well-trained horse. Good cutting horses now bring high prices and the sport is infiltrating into eastern states.

In the West, the horse is staging a comeback as a pleasure animal. The Palomino, with its golden color and light mane and tail, is in high favor. Old breeds, such as the Appaloosa, are coming back into popularity. With the traffic congestion becoming more and more aggravated and aggravating on those western freeways, it is not surprising that people are turning to the relaxation of riding horses along desert trails.

The large-scale invasion of the deserts is a development of recent years. In contrast, the invasion of the great plains and prairies of the central part of the continent came early and was more complete. These seas of waving grass were comparatively easy to convert to the growing of corn and wheat. The soil was fertile and there were no forests to be removed. The great herds of

Whirling, pivoting, never turning tail to calf, horse guards gulf between dogie and herd.

buffalo, however, were removed with shocking thoroughness.

The original buffalo population was beyond belief. Nobody knows how many animals there were, but they ranged from Mexico to Canada's Great Slave Lake and from Pennsylvania to the Rocky Mountains. Early estimates placed their number anywhere from sixty to one hundred million. Their wanton extermination is a black page in American history. Millions of the big beasts were shot for their hides and tongues. Thousands were killed in the name of sport, their carcasses left rotting on the prairie. The slaughter was so great that for years men made their living gathering up the bones to be ground into fertilizer.

It doesn't seem possible, but in 1889 the late Dr. William T. Hornady, conservationist and first president of the American Bison Society, announced after a census that only 591 buffalo were left in the United States. Their numbers dropped even lower than that before the society, which was formed in 1905, started a campaign to save the buffalo. The wild ones were gone from the plains, so the New York Zoological Society presented fifteen animals to the Wichita National Game Preserve in Oklahoma. In 1913 they also sent fourteen to Wind Cave National Park, in South Dakota.

Calf lunges toward herd but horse is ready, spins to cut it off. PHOTOS BY HY PESKIN

The slaughter had extended far into Canada, but a few wood buffalo, larger and darker than the plains variety, had survived in the wilderness south of Great Slave Lake. It is estimated that this fugitive herd, at its lowest point, numbered no more than 300.

A herd of plains buffalo, made up of animals purchased from private owners in the United States, had been established at Wainwright National Park, in Alberta. In 1922, the Canadian government created Wood Buffalo National Park, a wild expanse in the region where the few wood buffalo had escaped the hunters. From 1925 to 1928, 6,673 plains buffalo were transferred from Wainwright to the new refuge, which covers 17,500 square miles and is the largest national park on the continent. The combined herds prospered and a recent census placed the buffalo population there at more than 15,000 head. In the United States, public and private herds total around 10,000. A few hundred more are scattered in foreign parks and zoos, bringing the world population of the American bison to between 25,000 and 30,000.

The relationship between the people and the buffalo is quite different now from what it was in the days of the great slaughter. Today the creature is looked upon as a spectacular reminder of   241

Cowboys and Indians abound
at National Appaloosa Horse Show
at Canby, Oregon. Once nearly
extinct, breed developed by
Nez Perce Indians, named by French
for Palouse River grazing grounds,
is enjoying surge of recent
popularity. PHOTOS BY JOHN BRYSON

242

bygone days when the country was untamed. Herds are managed and the excess animals are killed and processed for the market. In some places licensed hunting is permitted. Through years of living inside fenced pastures, buffalo in the United States have lost much of their wildness, although it is still not advisable to get cozy with a buffalo bull. A typical herd is that in Custer State Park, near Rapid City, South Dakota, which is maintained at around a thousand head, about all that the park's 72,000 acres of range can support. These buffalo have been photographed so much by park visitors that they seem to strike a noble pose whenever anybody comes along with a camera.

On one occasion, Harvey Lancaster, a tall, wiry park ranger, took me on an auto tour of the buffalo range. Before we reached the main herd we stopped to watch a man photographing a young bull. The buffalo posed for a couple of shots and then moved away with considerable dignity.

We had left the road and were cutting across grassy plains when we came upon a herd of some 150 head, just standing around doing nothing in particular. Lancaster drove the car right in among them and stopped. Their usual reaction was to stand thirty feet or so from the car, stare at us stolidly, and then turn their backs in a somewhat bored manner.

"They're a little shy today," the ranger said. "Sometimes they'll come right up and try to poke their heads in the car window."

"What would happen if I got out of the car?" I asked.

"They'd run off."

Sitting there in the middle of the herd we made buffalo talk for quite a while. The ranger said that sometimes the old cows get ornery, but that they had never had anybody injured.

"In winter when we're feeding them hay, they're just like cattle," he said. "All you have to do is blow your horn and they'll come from all directions."

My first sight of Canadian buffalo was with William Essex, superintendent of Wood Buffalo Park, as we flew over the herds 243 in a small plane. Here was a different picture. Beneath us, and reaching into the distance, was a lush, green prairie with tree-lined rivers snaking through it. Dotting this plain were herds of buffalo, numbering up to several hundred per herd. At other seasons they gather in herds of several thousand.

Lone bulls lay in their muddy wallows along the river banks and reddish-brown calves grazed with their mothers. The scene stretched away to the horizon and it was just such a sight that white men came upon when they first pushed across the continent.

On other flights we cruised over wooded country where buffalo grazed in the forest or wallowed in open glades. Passing over a forest fire we saw the animals standing quietly in the smoke not far from the blaze, obviously realizing that the smoke drove away the swarms of insects that infested the woods.

Later, William A. Fuller, mammalogist of the Canadian Wildlife Service, took me on a trip into the park by Jeep. As we drove along a seldom-used dirt road, buffalo rose from their wallows and trotted off into the woods. When two bulls started straight down the road, Fuller took after them. We kept right behind the two lunging animals, each of which weighed more than a ton, and the Jeep was doing just thirty miles an hour. Fuller said that is about as fast as buffalo can run.

Once we left the Jeep and sneaked up on a small herd grazing in a slough. Hiding behind some small willows, we got within 150 feet of the nearest animals. As we stood there, an old bull would turn occasionally to stare in our direction. He must have seen us, but we were downwind and he found nothing alarming in a scientist and a reporter. We watched them for half an hour and then slipped away. Fuller explained that many of the buffalo in this huge preserve had never seen a human being.

Associated with the buffalo on the great plains was that curious animal, the prairie dog. Although not as imposing as the buffalo, these little short-tailed rodents far outnumbered them. Once the western plains supported prairie dogs in hosts now hard to visualize. They lived in deep burrows whose entrances were surrounded by mounds of earth. When not dining on prairie grasses, they sat upright on these mounds and barked.

Dr. C. H. Merriam, a noted and trustworthy naturalist, wrote in the Department of Agriculture Year Book of 1901 that, "Colonies twenty to thirty miles in length are not rare and in Texas one is known which measures about 250 miles one way and 100 to 150 the other, covering an area of about 25,000 square miles. It is certainly a conservative estimate to assume the average number of animals to be twenty-five per acre. On this assumption, the number of prairie dogs in the great Texas colony must be at least 400 million."

But agriculture and prairie dogs were not compatible. It has been estimated that 256 of the critters eat as much grass as one cow. Furthermore, their burrows were a hazard to livestock. Under a government program of poisoning and gassing, the dogs were exterminated throughout most of their range. The city of Lubbock now rests on the site of a great prairie-dog town.

Kennedy N. Clapp, a far-sighted resident of Lubbock, decided back in 1938 that some of the prairie dogs should be saved. Over the years he evolved Lubbock's famed prairie dog town. Now some 500 of these prolific relatives of the woodchuck live in a six-acre enclosure in Mackenzie Park, which is within the city limits. Although Lubbock lies off the main migration route of the tourists, travelers divert their cars 250 miles or more just to see the romping residents of Prairie Dog Town.

It took years before Clapp learned how to keep the prairie

Wantonly slain by early settlers, huge plains-buffalo population barely escaped extinction. Through careful preservation, remaining herds prospered and American bison are now plentiful enough to make limited hunting possible. PHOTO BY DAVID GOODNOW

dogs fenced. They kept digging out and starting new towns in unexpected places. Some of them escaped and went down to the golf course where they dug two holes right on one of the greens. There were loud protests from the golfing fraternity and prairie dog stock sank to a new low. Clapp experimented with various types of fencing, but escapes still were common. Small volcanoes of earth would appear outside the fences. Ranchers and farmers reported new dog diggings from one to three miles away.

Further research proved that the best fencing was heavy steel mesh buried in the ground. It developed that a prairie dog will dig under a wall, but when it meets mesh wire it becomes confused and digs elsewhere. Now there is a cinder block wall surrounding the dog town, with wire mesh below it. There have been no recent escapes and everybody is happy.

Lubbock is proud of this former scourge of the high plains and the local Chamber of Commerce describes it as "the lovable rodent." Pete the Prairie Dog festoons city brochures as he invites the world to come and share in the glories of Lubbock. Above the unique display is a sign which reads: "Prairie Dog Town. Population? $500 Fine for Molesting Prairie Dogs."

The buffalo has been saved and the prairie dog is confined behind cement and steel. There is a movement on foot to provide a suitable habitat for them on what was their former range. Other types of habitat have been preserved. There are national parks and national monuments containing deserts, forests, swamps, and mountains. But no large expanse of typical prairie country has been placed under protection.

Advocates of the plan feel that a large tract of land, at least one million acres, should be set aside for the preservation of typical prairie grasses and other plants and animals of the plains. Permitted to return to its original state such an area would be of great scientific value for comparative purposes. It would provide a place where the buffalo and the prairie dog could live in more natural surroundings, and new generations of Americans could see the 250 plains as their ancestors saw them.

Pleasure and production meet on Nebraska plains. Golfers and wheat farmer pause to chat where verdant fairway adjoins farmer's rippling yellow fields. PHOTO BY RICHARD MEEK

251

The scientific sea yields only to those who rigorously observe the discipline of its ways

SALT

WATER

Magnificently sweeping curves of ocean racers' hulls are exposed in drydock during spring overhaul at City Island boat yard on Long Island Sound. Deep-water sailers such as this 57-foot sloop (foreground) and lovely staysail schooner (rear) are queens of boating world. PHOTO BY RONNY JAQUES

The sea has always lured men to adventurous exploits. It led the early explorers in their clumsy caravels to the New World. It led Captain Joshua Slocum into the greatest of all sailing feats when he voyaged around the world alone in the thirty-six-foot yawl, *Spray.* In answer to the call of the sea men have endured bitter hardships and have gone back for more. Each year finds venturesome souls challenging the sea in all manner of precarious craft, from tiny sailboats to rafts.

It may be that the very vastness of the oceans is part of the attraction they have for the spirited and the daring. An appreciation of the emptiness and loneliness of the Atlantic was brought home to me during World War II when I was aboard a ship that picked up a lifeboat containing eighteen men from an American freighter that had been torpedoed by a submarine. The seamen told how they had sat in the drifting boat for thirty-two days, scanning the sea with dwindling hope. In all those thirty-two days they saw only two signs of human life—once when an empty whiskey bottle floated by and again when the periscope of another submarine slid past them through the calm sea.

Another fascination of the sea is its limitless power, the

energy incorporated in the tides, the currents, the force of the wind and storm-driven waves. Blue-water sailors don't go hunting for storms, but if you listen in on their conversation you will find that a large part of it concerns the storms they have weathered.

The size of the sea, its power, and even its loneliness—these plus the zest of competition are the ingredients that make ocean racing one of the finest of all sports. Each summer, fleets of yachts under clouds of canvas set out from the American mainland in races which take them across hundreds of miles of blue water. These are occasions of great nautical tradition and formality. The contenders set sail with spectator boats, sometimes numbering in the hundreds, following them for a time to wish them good luck in grand style. The competing yachts soon spread out over a wide area as each vessel tries to find the most favoring winds.

During a long race, the yachts are out of sight of each other and check their relative positions each day by radio. After the boats have arrived at their destination comes the involved application of the handicap rules, for in this type of competition the race does not always go to the first boat across the finish line. Once the race has ended there is always the round of parties and receptions at local yacht clubs.

The outstanding event on the East Coast is the Bermuda Race, oldest blue-water race in the country. In this biannual race, the skippers take their yachts from Newport, Rhode Island, for 635 miles across the Gulf Stream, where squalls often play havoc with the smaller craft. The Bermuda Race was first held in 1906. In recent years it has attracted more than a hundred boats.

On the West Coast, the premier ocean racing event is the Transpacific Race, a voyage from Los Angeles across 2,230 miles of open water to Honolulu. In 1959, this race attracted forty-one boats. Numerous other deep-water races reach out from both 258 coasts. Not all of them feature long distances. An overnight sail

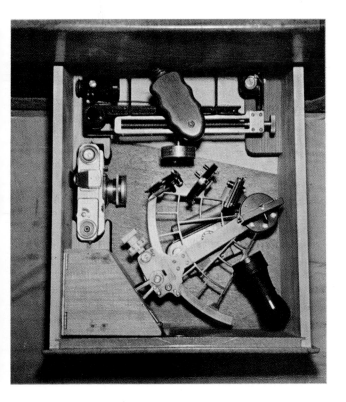

Looking aft from sleeping area, navigator's alcove is at left, behind bulkhead. Ladder leads to cockpit. Galley is at right.

Spectacularly canted deck of ocean racer about to tack is, as every sailor knows, a wondrous place to be. PHOTO BY DAVID KITZ

of only 124 miles, the Swiftsure Race, is one of the country's roughest. It starts and finishes at Brotchie Ledge off Victoria, British Columbia, with the Swiftsure Bank Lightship as the turn-around point. Squalls, racing tides, forty-knot headwinds, and consistently rough weather in the Straits of Juan de Fuca make this springtime event a race for those who don't mind punishment with their sport.

Ocean racing is an expensive sport that can be shared by only a few of the boating fraternity. This doesn't mean that all other boats are confined to bays. Hosts of smaller cruising craft, both power and sail, ply salt water along the coastlines. The very act of sailing a boat is a satisfaction in itself and the joys of cruising in your own boat are manifold.

The deep-sea sport fishermen have their own approach to blue water. Their idea of a fine craft is one designed for taking big fish. Like the yachtsmen, they follow a ritual and code of their own. Their tournaments are conducted under strict rules and protocol includes the flying of pennants to indicate what big fish has been caught. I know one man who undergoes a course of physical training to get himself in shape for a tuna tournament.

Ocean racing, cruising, deep-sea fishing, and voyages aboard commercial ships are the traditional sports and recreations of the sea. But since World War II another dimension to salt-water recreation for the average citizen has been added. This is skin diving. In the beginning phases of the sport, a simple diving mask and then the snorkel breathing tube enabled men to probe beneath the water's surface. What they found in the shallows and in the rich and colorful life of the reefs was so exciting that they strug-   263

Florida's Tampa Bay area has been sailed, it seems, by half the nation's sailors. Water is very blue, sea breezes are balmy, and round of regattas attracts boats from as far away as Kansas. Yawls pictured here are starting St. Petersburg ocean race. PHOTO BY JACK RAMSDELL

gled to go deeper, stay down longer, and see more.

Their efforts culminated during World War II, when the "scuba" appeared. "Scuba" means self-contained underwater breathing apparatus—the air tanks, harness, valves, mask, and mouthpiece that enable a diver to explore at length the natural environment of the creatures of the sea. It made accessible a new world of sport, adventure, and exploration.

It wasn't long before skin diving was a major activity with hundreds of thousands of addicts. Addicts is the proper word because there is something about skin diving that arouses an intense desire to spend as much time under water as possible. Men and women, not all of them young, prowl the sea floor as long as their air supply will let them. In southern California, where skin divers are legion, some groups have taken to exploring the bottom at night with flashlights. One form of this sport is the picnic which is held partly under water and partly on land. The couples meet on the beach and build a bonfire, then go below to hunt rock lobsters with their flashlights. Back ashore, they cook the lobsters on the bonfire and proceed to feast.

Along with skin diving came spear fishing. To the horror of traditional fishermen the skin divers went right into the water after the fish, pursuing them with spears propelled by rubber thongs, springs, or carbon-dioxide guns. The hook-and-line fishermen shuddered and predicted disaster.

In many places these new hunters of the deep overdid it. They killed fish just for the fun of it. They took far more than they needed and they depleted cherished fishing spots of the fishermen above. In some places off the Florida Keys, a group would spend the day cleaning out most of the fish around a coral head, then haul away their catch and sell it at cut-rate prices to help defray   267

Plunging downwind with spinnakers flying, racers on Long Island Sound are inevitably beautiful. PHOTO BY MORRIS ROSENFELD

the expenses of their trip.

Such practices led to war between the traditional anglers and the spear fishermen. In some places local waters were closed to spear fishing. In others the feud goes on. Some persons interested in the sport feel that spear fishing will have to be regulated by law if it is to thrive.

It would never have to be regulated if all spear fishermen adhered to the self-imposed rules followed by the Pinder brothers —Don, Fred, and Art—of Florida, who have won many spear-fishing championships, including the national. Rule One: edible fish should be taken with a fair idea of the ultimate consumer, and not in the vague hope that it can be passed on to a neighbor. Rule Two: the rare and beautiful fish of relatively little food value should be left alone. Rule Three: once a fish is speared, the hunter must not spear another until he has retrieved his catch or exhausted all chance of doing so.

Spearing fish is not the sole aim of skin divers. Underwater photography has become an adjunct of the sport, as camera equipment has improved along with diving gear. Art McKee, of Treasure Harbor, Florida, has had considerable success probing offshore waters for treasure and ancient relics from the wrecks of Spanish galleons. Skin divers like to explore reefs, caves, and grottoes, watching the sea life about them as a bird watcher studies his birds. A more specialized group goes in for exploration and photography at depths of 200 feet or more. This takes them into an even stranger world of half-light and big fish.

Underwater activity has been recognized by cartoonists as a new part of the American scene and magazines are beginning to look for laughs in such situations as the entanglement of skin divers in trawlers' nets.

All this is not so far-fetched as it might seem. Conrad Limbaugh, diver for the Scripps Oceanographic Institution, at La Jolla, California, once had an elephant seal come up behind him and start chewing on his helmet. Peter R. Gimbel, who has explored many offshore depths with his friend, Michael Gaynor, 269 described one curious but terrifying experience as follows:

"We were exploring a place called Cox Ledge, about thirty-five miles east of Montauk Point. Cox Ledge is actively fished by the party boats out of Connecticut and Montauk Point. On this occasion we dived to a depth of 130 feet, orienting our descent by following the anchor line of the party boat *Mijoy*. We soon came upon a very strange sight indeed.

"A cluster of half a dozen or more fishhooks temptingly baited were jerking up and down near the bottom, their leaden sinkers plunking into the sand. Several fish were very much interested in the baits, and we saw one cod get hooked and go struggling up into the gray light of the middle ground between the other lines that looked like slender and mysterious filaments suspended through a fog. I became so intrigued with this scene that before I realized it I was in the very midst of the wildly jerking hooks and almost instantly was hooked in three or four places. Holding the camera, which I was not willing to release and risk losing in the poor light, I began slowly to rise with the upward pulling hooks. I was more than a little worried by the suddenly chaotic turn of things. Michael, who was not encumbered by carrying anything and who had sized up the situation almost before it developed, was with me in an instant and had me free in a few seconds. However, he was soon hooked himself and, while he was busy removing the steel from his hide, my face mask was suddenly yanked from my face, leaving me blind. This, of course, was serious. I reached desperately above my head and luckily grabbed the mask, which I pulled free of the hook and flushed dry with a great snort of relief. Michael meanwhile had got himself loose and we hastily swam out of the angling range of the *Mijoy* in considerable awe, if not downright fear, of the effectiveness of her fishermen."

270

PAGE 272 : *Foul-weather gear is needed on board heeling sloop in typically wild wet sailing on San Francisco Bay.* PHOTO BY ROBERT LACKENBACH

PAGE 273 : *Competitor is half hidden by surging Pacific during Swiftsure race, roughest sailing event in United States.* PHOTO BY KENNETH G. OLLAR

Dauntless fishermen (right) urge small boat through whirlpools and breakers off Westport, Washington, in pursuit of king salmon. PHOTO BY BURT GLINN

Sailfish (left) catapults high out of blue, blue Pacific waters off coast of Mexico while harnessed angler keeps line taut. PHOTO BY JACK BIRNS

The other end of this story must have been a curious one, too. I can hear the fishermen now, telling in wild excitement about the big one that got away. Suppose that Gimbel had not been able to free himself and the fishermen had hauled him to the surface. Would they have demanded the right to keep their catch?

With such things already happening as the result of this mass movement under the waves, it is not difficult to look into the future of skin diving. More devices will be developed to increase man's freedom beneath the sea. Suits will be devised enabling him to withstand greater pressures and thus reach greater depths. Gadgets with propellers, some of which are already being used, will take explorers greater distances.

I can see the day when guides will take parties of sightseers through caves and caverns and to scenic spots on the ocean floor. Beneath the waters just outside New York harbor lies a mighty canyon which is an underwater extension of the Hudson River gorge. If this feature could be raised above the surface it would be a prime scenic wonder. That, of course, is impossible, but in time exploring parties equipped with lights undoubtedly will be led through this ocean canyon by competent guides.

With the undersea gardens so heavily populated, it will be necessary to set aside national parks and monuments to preserve

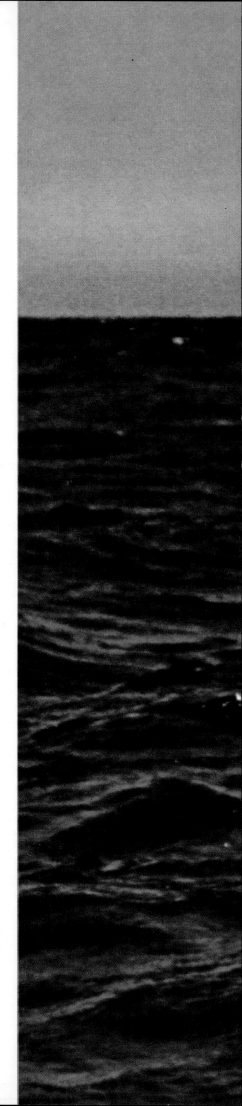

Supreme moment for deep-sea fisherman comes when giant black marlin erupts from sea in white cloud of foam. This 500-pounder made 14 leaps in furious 30-minute battle. PHOTO BY CORNELL CAPA

276

Treasure hunters dislodge 3,000-pound cannon from decayed wreckage of Spanish galleon. This is work for experienced divers, but such sites may one day be underwater museums. PHOTO BY PETER STACKPOLE

our watery wonders. Ancient wrecks may be fenced off and protected in underwater preserves so that generations of skin-diving
tourists may enjoy them. You may think this is going a bit far,
but consider that the Bahamian government already is in the
process of establishing an undersea park down in the region of
the Exhuma Cays, and that along the coast of California people
are seeking means of legislating ocean preserves to protect the
assets of the deep.

Since the establishment of the big oceanariums in Florida and
California, it has been discovered that some of the mammals of
the sea have far more intelligence and react more favorably to
association with man than anyone had realized. Scientists engaged in research have discovered some astonishing things about
the porpoise and new facets of the lives of these playful creatures
are being unfolded constantly. At Marineland of the Pacific, in
California, they have found that pilot whales can be as playful
as porpoises and can be taught all sorts of tricks.

Porpoises have been taught to leap high out of the water to
take a fish from a man's hand. They have learned to ring bells,
hoist flags, speak for food, and play all sorts of games. In response
to human companionship they have proved friendly and even
affectionate. When fed by a diver who enters their tank they are
respectful, taking fish from his hand and each waiting its turn.
They love to be petted, tickled, and scratched and will raise their
heads above the water to be patted.

Although they live underwater, they are able to communi-
cate with each other by a great variety of sounds. They can hear
and emit sounds too high pitched to be caught by the human ear.
A porpoise's hearing ranges up to 100,000 cycles per second, while
280 the average human ear can handle only about 20,000 cps.

PAGES 282-283: *Wonders of underwater* *exploration are displayed by spear* *fisherman (left) and Clare Booth Luce.* PHOTOS BY ED FISHER AND COLES PHINIZY

Coral reefs are home and hunting grounds *of odd and beautiful fish such as* *ruby-eyed squirrelfish (left), queen* *angelfish (above).* PHOTOS BY DAVID GOODNOW

In our look into the future of skin diving, it is not hard to see porpoises being reared and trained in oceanarium tanks as aquatic pets. Then when divers go for long strolls along the bottom of the sea they can take their trained porpoises along as pets and companions.

Through his inventive genius, man has made available to himself an ancient but little-known world. There is no reason to believe that he will not continue to penetrate these fascinating deeps and learn their ways, even as he has discovered much about his planet and a little bit about the universe in which it moves. The seas and oceans of the world are now under more intensive study and exploration than they ever have been before. It is to be hoped that past experiences on land will lead to wiser use and better conservation of this newly opened realm of the outdoors.   285

*Land encircled
by water is, by all the
rules, enchanted*

ISLANDS

Surfboard riding, original sport of the Hawaiians and long associated with their islands, is now being practiced by eager tourists

ho quickly learn to balance themselves atop rollers that sweep in from the ocean to wash the shimmering sands. PHOTO BY HY PESKIN

*I should like to rise and go
Where the golden apples grow,
Where beneath some other sky
Parrot islands anchored lie
And watched by cockatoos and goats
Lonely Crusoes building boats.*
        Robert Louis Stevenson

Why a piece of land surrounded by water should have special distinction is hard to say. But beyond question, in the hearts and minds of everyone who ever permitted himself a daydream, it does. The island suggests adventure, implies romance, and encourages self-reliance. The island visitor enters the world of Lord Jim and Ginger Ted, of sly John Silver and the prim, do-it-yourself Robinsons, of Gauguin, Darwin, Emile de Becque and the men of the *Bounty*. How easy it is to project them on the wide screen of the mind's eye. And having done so, to find oneself amongst them, to hear the lookout's cry, attend the landfall, bend to the oar, wade up the beach, to become pirate, planter, whaler, beachcomber—or 290 perpetual vacationer.

These are among the visions that islands stir in those who visit them. An island is an entity, a complete thing that can be tucked away and remembered as one would remember a poem or the tune of a well-loved song. Islands demand exploration. And once explored they become a possession. Those who have visited an island look upon it ever after with a proprietary interest. Permanent residents of the island, who invariably have an intense sense of ownership themselves, may seethe at such mental larceny, but perhaps it is one of the very special things about islands. Once experienced they can be taken away, yet, at the same time, left there for others.

Small-scale maps of the United States fail to show many islands, but a closer scrutiny of our coastline reveals thousands of them: some large, some small; some rocky and tree-covered, like those sprinkled along the leading edge of Maine; some long, low and sandy. Some are pinnacles rising from the watery plain of the sea and others, like those of southern Florida, are built of old coral and clothed with a mysterious tangle of mangrove jungle. No two are the same. Each has a unique character.

Traditional vacation islands lying off northern coasts are host to masses of mainlanders during the summer, and in winter the southern islands swarm with midwesterners. Thousands more seek the pleasant isles of the Bahamas and the great variety of lures provided by the West Indies.

And when they put that fiftieth star in the flag it meant that in Hawaii the nation had acquired not only a new state, but one composed entirely of islands. Their fascination is long-lived, has been extolled since Captain Cook dropped anchor there in 1778. Now, statehood and airplanes, including speedy jets, have made them even more attractive and accessible to the mainlander.

More than 160,000 vacationers journey to the fiftieth state each year, drawn there by the promised "charm of the islands." To the majority, this "charm" means dancing girls in grass skirts, waving palms, vivid sunsets, mountain rainbows and surf riders. In recent years, though, more and more travelers are discovering that the islands provide much interest and excitement beyond the surface enchantments so thoroughly advertised.

Most of the sports indulged in by Hawaiians have been imported. But there is one that is original, an invention requiring only a wooden slab and the long rollers that sweep in from the Pacific. Captain Cook and his men were astonished to find the natives scurrying to sea on boards, then sliding back on a boiling wave. The fame of this spectacular way of enjoying nature has become world-wide. Coles Phinizy, *Sports Illustrated's* expert on the Hawaiian Islands, has this to say about the status of wave riding and of Robert "Rabbit" Keki, one of its greatest practitioners:

"Today the man on the surfboard next to Rabbit Keki may be another islander or he may be a one-hundred-per-cent tourist from Waukegan, Illinois, fifty years old, ashamed of his paunch, and so surprised to find himself standing on a wave that he shouts futilely to his wife ashore for God's sake look quick.

"At Waikiki, Rabbit Keki has taught surfboarding to over 5,000 visitors. Several years ago Keki taught two gentle seventy-year-old ladies from Minnesota to stand on a board in their first lesson. The picture of them lingers in his mind—two ladies standing stiff and gaunt-legged as blue herons, shrilling with glee as they slide to shore—and it has confounded Keki ever since that hundreds of thousands of tourists never try the sport. Keki and other instructors estimate that not one in fifty visitors tries surf-

294

Future explorers of moon may well
encounter landscape similar to cindery,
rock-studded plains of quiescent
crater of Haleakala (left) on Maui.
Water skier (below) ruffles
waters of Wailua River, winding through
Kauai to sea. PHOTOS BY TONI FRISSELL

boarding, though certainly one out of every two could learn enough in one lesson to get a taste of it. Without trying, many visitors conclude they cannot learn. Too many are inhibited, coming to the islands in the thrall of an unfortunate mainland belief that any sportsman over thirty who does not have a physique like Sandow should confine himself to dog paddling, occasional tennis, and a slow death of weekend golf.

"Good Hawaiian board riders have been clocked at over thirty miles an hour as they are angling—'sliding,' as it is commonly known—on the shoulder of a wave. The sport in the ultimate, like skiing, requires footwork and finesse in shifting the body weight—fine points that Waikiki instructors are willing to teach anyone who wants more than a few lessons. The beginner who tries too many tricks prematurely at Waikiki should bear in mind that outrigger canoes have the right of way on the wave, and that the coral under the water does not move for anybody."

On leaving the famed beaches to seek the interior of the islands, visitors find plenty to do and all of it in a spectacular setting. It is one thing to swim in a pool, but the swim becomes a richer experience if that pool is at the foot of a towering waterfall. Hunters find themselves seeking their game on misty mountains festooned with rainbows. The game in the islands is an odd assortment of imported species: feral sheep, goat and pig, axis deer, California Valley and Japanese quail, barred and lace-neck doves, ringnecked pheasant, chukar partridge, and wild pigeon.

On the slopes of Mauna Kea, on the big island of Hawaii, public hunting grounds reach from an elevation of 6,000 feet up over the rough, volcanic summit at 13,800 feet. On the island of Lanai, the hunter seeks the spotted axis deer and the small Japanese quail. The public hunting grounds of Hawaii and Maui pro-

vide chukar and pheasant, and the island of Molokai is best for Valley quail. All are hunted amid scenes of wild beauty.

In like manner, fishermen seek 300-pound marlin off the Kona coast, with the volcano, Mauna Loa, rising as a backdrop, and on Kauai bonefish are caught by casting from jagged bluffs bathed in spray. No matter what sport or diversion the visitor seeks, he can never forget that his playground is the result of some of the mightiest upheavals the earth has ever experienced. From a base of about 15,000 feet below the sea, a series of eruptions built the islands up to a maximum height of 13,823 feet above.

An appreciation of the might of those primordial forces comes to all visitors who make the trip into the crater of Haleakala, which rises 10,025 feet on the island of Maui. Here they find not only some of the more awesome charms of the islands, but also get an idea of what the surface of the moon undoubtedly will look like when we get there. Come to think of it, the moon is a sort of an island, surrounded by space instead of water.

For most of his life Frank Freitas, a Portuguese trail rider, has guided parties of visitors on horseback up the trail that clings to the side of a thousand-foot cliff and through the weird landscape inside the crater. Dotting the fifteen square miles of the crater floor are cinder cones, 400 to 900 feet high, left there by lesser eruptions in the past, and the cindery plains are sprinkled with basalt statuary cast by the fires of the volcano.

Pushing out from the east coast of the United States, vacationers explore a wealth of tropic islands from Bermuda to Bonaire, a lonely gem lying off the coast of Venezuela. When we think of Bermuda, it is usually in terms of the five main islands, but clustering around them are 300 islets, boasting the world's northernmost coral reefs. Few American vacationists get to

301

Breath-taking sight of thousands of wild flamingos rising in flight may be seen in lonely parts of world where great, colorful bir

make home. Ascent is chaotic scramble of awkward bodies and beating wings, but once air-borne, flamingos possess majestic beauty.

Bonaire, but those who do—and at the right season of the year—are rewarded by one of nature's grandest sights: a mass of flamingos wheeling beneath a bright blue sky.

Flamingos build their mud cities and rear their young in some of the loneliest places on earth. Ornithologists who have crossed the mucky flats which form the barrier to most flamingo nesting grounds say there is nothing more impressive in the bird world than to see several thousand flamingos as they clamber into the sky. In a mighty tangle of wings, legs, and long necks, the birds thunder aloft. The scarlet of their massed bodies is punctuated by the black of their flight feathers. Their odd shape, vibrant color, and stately flight create a blend of the bizarre and the beautiful.

There are other colonies of American flamingos, including one at Inagua, in the Bahamas, where the birds are strictly protected. Most travelers consider themselves lucky if they get a glimpse of even a few of the wild birds moving through a vista of sea and sky. A closer look at captive flamingos can be obtained near Nassau, on New Providence Island, and, of course, there is the famed captive breeding colony surrounded by the Hialeah Racetrack. When the horses are not running, tourists go there just to see flamingos.

Deserted flamingo community on Bonaire, N.W.I.,
resembles ruins of ancient city. Nest mounds are made
of rolled pellets of mud, piled high to keep
egg or young bird safe from shallow tides on flats.

In the seas between Bermuda on the north and Bonaire on the south are countless islands waiting to be explored. Ranging in size from Cuba to a coral rock, they swing in a great, diversified chain, curving from the Florida peninsula all the way down to Trinidad, just off the coast of Venezuela.

For those who lean toward history and adventure it is enough to know that many of these islands lie along the Spanish Main, the route through the Caribbean taken by the Spanish treasure galleons, that many of them were the haunts of pirates, and that they include San Salvador, the spot where Columbus made his landfall in the New World on October 12, 1492. Included, too, are the United States possessions, Puerto Rico and the Virgin Islands.

Improvements here are in large part due to Laurance Rockefeller, who, like his four brothers, devotes much of his time, energy, and money to intelligent philanthropy. No stranger to the Caribbean and the Bahamas, Rockefeller bought Caneel Bay Plantation, on St. John, the least populous of the three Virgins, and spent some $4 million developing it into one of the handsomest beach resorts in the world. He was so impressed by the beauty of the island that he bought up 5,000 acres, about half of the island, and offered it to the Federal government as a national park. It was accepted and in December, 1956, it became the twenty-ninth scenic recreation area administered by the National Park Service.

He also became convinced that an excellent way to bolster the economy of Puerto Rico would be to build a first-class resort area to attract more tourists to the island for extended visits.

To this end he purchased 1,200 acres of land along the coast at Dorado and built a resort area with a magnificent golf course as its focal point. Here golfers play four holes along the ocean front and the rest of the course inland, through grapefruit groves and   305

Focal point of Laurance Rockefeller's new Dorado Beach resort in Puerto Rico is superb golf course running parallel to ocean and

through green jungle clearings. Resort's rambling design makes most of coastline, insures guests' privacy. PHOTO BY EZRA STOLLER

jungle clearings. Beside the golf course, there are cottages, a hotel, tennis courts, horse-drawn victorias, and two beaches.

Such tropic isles as these are generally the goal of winter vacationers. When summer heat waves shimmer across the corn belt, the migration to the more traditional vacation islands hard by the northern coasts begins. The most famous of these old stand-bys is Nantucket, a small island with a long history, located twenty-five miles south of Cape Cod. In summertime, Nantucket is a busier place than it was in the days when its fleet of 150 ships searched the seas for whales. Its population swells to as much as 25,000. By winter, however, it is down to about 3,000.

In time, habitual visitors often come to regard the island as their own, but their claims are never acknowledged by a true, bred-in-the-bone islander. Gerald Holland, a student of Nantucket sociometrics, illustrates the immutable pecking order of the island as follows:

"One time, years ago, an infant was carried ashore at Nantucket on a pillow. The baby was two weeks old. His parents decided to settle permanently, and the child grew up and went to school and on to high school and then into business. He became an outstanding citizen. He was active in civic affairs and in church work. As he prospered, he gave generously to all local charities and was on every committee anybody could think up. He had a long and fruitful life and he lived to be ninety-six years of age. The church was filled for the funeral service and when the preacher got up to deliver the eulogy, he began by saying, 'Brethren, we are gathered here today to pay our last respects to a beloved stranger.' "

The island which brings the "strangers" back year after year is an odd mixture of sand and history. There are some sizable trees in the towns, but the open parts of the island support little more than scrub oak and dwarf pine. What it lacks in trees it makes up for in flowers. White daisies, red wild roses, broom and heather bloom in profusion.

308   Despite its unspectacular terrain—the highest hill is only

*"Bright Day, Bathers," by Arthur
B. Davies, hangs in Addison Gallery of
American Art at Andover, Massachusetts.
Millions at seashore revel in
simple pleasures of rolling surf
and relaxation under warm summer skies.*

ninety-one feet—the island offers plenty of diversion. It is bounded by fine beaches and is favored by surfcasters, male and female. Visitors to Nantucket swim and sail, search the beaches for seashells and driftwood, ride horseback, picnic, paint pictures, snap pictures, hike, bike, play golf, play tennis, play a highly scientific game of croquet, watch birds, band birds, take historical tours, or browse through the museums and libraries.

In 1659, Thomas Mayhew sold the greater part of the island of Nantucket for thirty pounds and two beaver hats. There came a time after the death of the whaling industry when some would

309

have considered the price about right. It took the American vacationist to prove that the island had greater values than those gained by chasing whales.

There is still another type of island for which Americans constantly search. This is the undiscovered, uninhabited, or "unspoiled" island. It may be a large one or a mere rock. I know a man in Florida who frequently visits an island which has a diameter of only about fifty feet. It has one buttonwood tree and a few bushes. This man likes to sit there for an hour or two, watching the boats plying a channel not far away. He says it gives him a good feeling just to be alone on "his" island.

I was in luck when I became a member of an expedition sent out by the Scripps Institution of Oceanography at La Jolla, California, to explore Guadalupe Island, off the Mexican coast. Our party was led by Professor Carl L. Hubbs, the eminent biologist, and included scientists from the Scripps Institution and the San Diego Museum of Natural History. Our objective was a natural history survey of the island, one of the world's wildest. I'll never forget my first view of it.

Dead ahead and towering above the low-lying mists of the morning were dark and rocky headlands. As our stubby ship, the *Orca,* bore down on the island from the north, these grim promontories took on the tortured shapes and somber coloring of extinct volcanoes.

Those of us who had never visited Guadalupe Island before were utterly unprepared for the wild scenes revealed by the lifting haze. We had been so intrigued by accounts of the rediscovery of the Townsend fur seal, a creature often declared to be extinct, by the astonishing comeback of the elephant seals at this island haven, and by the promise of other unusual animals that we had formed no mental picture of the island itself. But here in the early sunlight was a grotesque volcanic mass rivaling the finest islands of fiction. The *Nautilus* might have been harbored here. Ben Gunn might have roamed those deep ravines. It was hard to keep in mind that we had sailed only 220 miles southwest from San Diego

310

and that Baja California was only 140 miles to the east.

Throughout most of its meager history, man has given Guadalupe Island a dirty deal. Early in the last century, Russian sealers brought Aleut Indians from Alaska to take fur seals by the hundreds of thousands. Names of ships and dates scratched on boulders indicate that the crews of Yankee ships from New England also shared in the slaughter. Volcanic rocks worn smooth by the sliding bodies of generations of fur seals give evidence to the numbers that once were there. The massive elephant seals were killed in like numbers for their blubber.

Whaling vessels put goats ashore more than a century ago, so they would increase and provide meat when the ships returned. The descendants of those goats have ravaged the native vegetation to the point where some plants are now extinct.

As the *Orca* eased to an anchorage in a cove near the north

Beach buggies transport summer visitors to Nantucket's diversions. PHOTO BY TONI FRISSELL

In hot summer months, inlanders migrate to vacation islands off northern coasts. Nantucket, south of Cape Cod, was once whaling center, is now thriving resort. PHOTOS BY TONI FRISSELL

end of the island, a chorus of sound came across the smooth expanse of water. Sometimes it seemed like distant carpenters at work, at others it sounded like a great pot boiling and bubbling.

It came from the shore, and through the glasses we determined that the dark masses along one stretch of beach were not boulders, but hundreds of elephant seals lolling on the sand and making the curious noises of their kind. On the slope behind them were deserted barracks where a Mexican garrison had been quartered during World War II. Now, a few Mexican marines maintain a weather station at the southern end of the twenty-two-mile island. They and their families are the only inhabitants.

No sooner had the anchor dropped into the blue water than small boats were put over the side to ferry the scientists, divers, and technicians to their selected tasks. This was the beginning of a week during which the island and its environs were subjected to study from the heights to the depths.

Eager to confront the elephant seals, Richard Meek, *Sports Illustrated* photographer, and I elected to be put ashore at one of their beaches. As we unloaded our gear wild goats grazed on the nearby slopes and in the distant highlands, which rise to almost 4,500 feet, we could see others. Some were mottled brown and black, some were white, others all black. There were big billies with long, curling horns and nannies followed by light-footed kids.

After watching the goats scramble up the cliffs, we crossed a dry wash, passed the stone ruins of sealers' shacks built more than a century ago, and climbed to a small ridge. Just beyond the ridge more than 200 elephant seals lay sprawled in the black sand. Climbing down, we approached the lazing herd. The closer we got the more we were inclined to laugh. Before the day was over we were to laugh a great deal.

Expedition members (above) cross to rocky islet off west coast of Guadalupe to study nesting birds. Hundreds of elephant seals gather on beach and frolic in ocean. PHOTOS RY RICHARD MEEK

Stretched out in postures of lassitude, the fat hulks seemed to have not a single care in the world. They ranged from youngsters five or six feet long to mighty bulls up to sixteen feet and weighing between 5,000 and 6,000 pounds. Their eyes were huge and above each eye was a ridiculous eyebrow composed of eight or ten bristles. Their mouths turned down with a solemnity that didn't seem to fit their comical physiques.

Occasionally, one would dig down with a flipper and toss black sand over its back. Here and there, one scratched deliberately with an arched flipper. Their faces and shapes were odd enough, but as nothing compared to the noises they made. They gargled, gurgled, and burped. They snorted and hissed, and their stomachs rumbled. Adult males inflated their sixteen-inch trunks, turned them back into their mouths, and made a loud "bop, bop, bop, bop," which sounded like a pile driver. It must be kept in mind that all these sounds were on a gargantuan scale, issued so lustily that the chorus reverberated through the adjacent canyons.

Beyond the prostrate elephant seals, others played in the surf. Their idea of play is to form a compact group and bounce up and down with the waves, biting each other as they bounce. They do this for hours, occasionally pausing to raise their heads in a resounding bellow or gargle.

As we sat on a boulder watching, it was hard to realize that this northern elephant seal, *Mirounga angustirostris,* had once been on the verge of extermination. Originally, the species flourished on a stretch of coast almost a thousand miles long and reaching north to San Francisco Bay. But by 1892, a whaling vessel visiting Guadalupe found only eight elephant seals. Crewmen killed seven of them. In 1922 an expedition found 264 adult males after the breeding season and since then the island has been a seal sanc-

tuary. Our expedition counted 2,117 elephant seals, but during the breeding season more than 10,000 have been found on the island.

Since their successful comeback on Guadalupe, the elephant seals are spreading northward again to the California coast, including one small group on South Coronado Island, only twenty-one miles from San Diego.

Our expedition also counted seventy-five Townsend fur seals swimming and playing among the rocks and in the caves of the ragged coastline. This species, a relative of the northern fur seal which breeds on the Pribilof Islands of the Bering Sea, was thought to have been wiped out by the sealers as early as 1830. Since then they had reappeared only to be virtually killed off again. The present small colony was discovered in 1954 and the scientists who make periodic checks hope that this time the seals will be able to make their comeback unmolested.

For a week, the members of our group combed the island for scientific treasures. They scaled the steep cliffs for rare plants. From 1,200 feet down in the dark blue water offshore their nets brought up lantern fish, which provide their own light in the primeval blackness, ruby-red shrimps, hatchetfish, and other oddities. Our skin divers explored grottoes and confronted the seals in their own element. We identified birds and watched the geysers of spray breaking on the crags of the western shore.

On the afternoon of our departure, the island staged a wild spectacle for us. Black storm clouds gathered over the highlands. Thunder rocked and rolled through the steep valleys and rain fell in a tropical deluge. Chocolate-colored rivulets were soon rattling down the ravines and tumbling over the cliffs in murky water-falls. The rivulets grew into cataracts plunging down the canyon with an increasing roar.

As our ship pulled away from the island the sky began to clear. The rumble of the flash floods drowned out the cries of the elephant seals along the beach. The murky, silt-laden water spread out over the sea and a rainbow arched over all.

In time, the island sank from view, but its ragged cliffs and valleys, the goats, the lazy, bellowing elephant seals, the young fur seals at play in the tide pools, and the violent beauty of the storm were still clear in our minds. And they still are. For it is a charac-teristic of islands, whether wild and raw like Guadalupe or old and settled in their ways like Nantucket, that once they have been experienced, they remain with you always.

If once you have slept on an island,
You'll never be quite the same;
You may look as you looked the day before
And go by the same old name.
You may hustle about in street and shop,
You may sit at home and sew,
But you'll see blue water and wheeling gulls
Wherever your feet may go....

                              Rachel Field
"Taxis and Toadstools," Doubleday and Co.

*Rich in beaches and birdsong, tropical vegetation, and aquatic pleasures,
St. John glows red in peaceful afternoon sun. Says developer
Laurance Rockefeller of this idyllic retreat:* "We bought something that
was good not knowing how good it was." PHOTO BY BRADLEY SMITH